Henry David Thoreau, H. G. O Blake

Thoreau's Thoughts

Selections from the Writings of Henry David Thoreau

Henry David Thoreau, H. G. O Blake

Thoreau's Thoughts
Selections from the Writings of Henry David Thoreau

ISBN/EAN: 9783744665896

Printed in Europe, USA, Canada, Australia, Japan

Cover: Foto ©Thomas Meinert / pixelio.de

More available books at **www.hansebooks.com**

THOREAU'S THOUGHTS

SELECTIONS FROM THE WRITINGS
OF HENRY DAVID THOREAU

EDITED BY

H. G. O. BLAKE

We shall one day see that the most private is the most public
energy, that quality atones for quantity, and grandeur of character
acts in the dark, and succors them who never saw it.

EMERSON

BOSTON AND NEW YORK
HOUGHTON, MIFFLIN AND COMPANY
The Riverside Press, Cambridge
1890

INTRODUCTORY.

In selecting the following passages from Thoreau's printed works, for the use of those who are already interested in him, and to win, if possible, new admirers of what has given me so pure and unfailing a satisfaction for now more than forty years, I desired to make a pocket volume, containing beautiful and helpful thoughts, which one might not only read in retirement, but use as a traveling companion, or *vade mecum*, while waiting at a hotel, railway station, or elsewhere, — something even more convenient and ready at hand than the newspaper. I would furnish an antidote to the dissipating, depressing influence of too much newspaper reading, something which instead of filling the mind with gos-

sip, political strife and misstatement, ath-
letics, pugilism, accounts of shocking acci-
dents, and every kind of criminality, may
refresh us with a new sense of the beauty
of the world, and make us feel how truly
life is worth living.

> " O world as God has made it, all is beauty ;
> And knowing this is love, and love is duty."

The truth expressed in these lines of
Browning, which seems to me the highest
wisdom, and so the essence of religion, was
no transient dream with Thoreau, but a
deep conviction which took possession of
him early in life, never to be relinquished,
and which he resolved as far as possible
to realize, in spite of the false usages and
allurements of the ' world as ' man ' has
made it.' Though, faithful to his idea, he
felt obliged to stand somewhat apart from
the society about him, yet his strong and
active interest in the anti-slavery move-
ment, and his instant appreciation and
public defense of Captain John Brown,
show clearly how sensitive he was to the

tie of humanity. It is the close alliance
or unity of Thoreau's genius and personal
character which gives such power to his
words for the purpose I have in view,
namely, to awaken or revive our interest
in the worthiest things, to lift us above the
world of care and sadness into that fairer
world which is always waiting to receive us.

I would express here my obligations to
Dr. Samuel A. Jones, of Ann Arbor, Michigan, for the free use of his "Bibliography," which has been with him indeed
a labor of love, and which, I am sure, will
add much to the value and attractiveness
of this volume.

THE EDITOR.

SELECTIONS FROM THOREAU.

The best kind of reading.   Reading, in a high sense, is not that which lulls us as a luxury and suffers the nobler faculties to sleep the while, but what we have to stand on tiptoe to read and devote our most alert and wakeful hours to.   WALDEN, p. 113.

Society in solitude.   I have never felt lonesome, or in the least oppressed by a sense of solitude, but once, and that was a few weeks after I came to the woods, when, for an hour, I doubted if the near neighborhood of man was not essential to a serene and healthy life. To be alone was something unpleasant. But I was at the same time conscious of a slight insanity in my mood, and seemed to foresee my recovery. In the midst of a gentle rain, while these thoughts prevailed, I was suddenly sensible of such sweet and beneficent society in Nature, in the very pattering of the

drops, and in every sound and sight around
my house, an infinite and unaccountable
friendliness all at once like an atmosphere
sustaining me, as made the fancied advan-
tages of human neighborhood insignificant,
and I have never thought of them since.
Every little pine needle expanded and
swelled with sympathy and befriended me.
I was so distinctly made aware of the presence of something kindred to me, even in
scenes which we are accustomed to call
wild and dreary, and also that the nearest
of blood to me and humanest was not a
person nor a villager, that I thought no
place could ever be strange to me again.

WALDEN, p. 143.

The best
neighbor-
hood.   What sort of space is that which
separates a man from his fellows
and makes him solitary ? I have found that
no exertion of the legs can bring two minds
much nearer to one another.   What do we
want most to dwell near to ? Not to
many men surely, the depot, the post-of-
fice, the bar-room, the meeting-house, the
school-house, the grocery, Beacon Hill, or
the Five Points, where men most congre-
gate, but to the perennial source of our

life, whence in all our experience we have found that to issue, as the willow stands near the water and sends out its roots in that direction. This will vary with different natures, but this is the place where a wise man will dig his cellar.   WALDEN, P. 144.

Our nearest neighbor.   Any prospect of awakening or coming to life to a dead man makes indifferent all times and places. The place where that may occur is always the same, and indescribably pleasant to all our senses. For the most part we allow only outlying and transient circumstances to make our occasions. They are, in fact, the cause of our distraction. Nearest to all things is that power which fashions their being. *Next* to us the grandest laws are continually being executed. *Next* to us is not the workman whom we have hired, with whom we love so well to talk, but the workman whose work we are.
                                    WALDEN, p. 145.

Our double nature.   However intense my experience, I am conscious of the presence and criticism of a part of me, which, as it were, is not a part of me, but spectator, sharing no experience, but taking note of it; and that is no more I than it is you. When the play, it may be the tragedy, of life is over, the spectator goes his way. It was a kind of fiction, a work of the imagination only, so far as he was concerned. This doubleness may easily make us poor neighbors and friends sometimes.

WALDEN, p. 146.

The most satisfactory companionship.

I never found the companion that was so companionable as solitude. We are for the most part more lonely when we go abroad among men than when we stay in our chambers.

WALDEN, p. 147.

Too much shallow intercourse.

Society is commonly too cheap. We meet at very short intervals, not having had time to acquire any new value for each other. We live thick and are in each other's way, and stumble over one another, and I think that we thus lose some respect for one another. Certainly less frequency would suffice for all important and hearty communications. The value of a man is not in his skin, that we should touch him.

WALDEN, p. 147.

The value of solitude. I have a great deal of company in my house; especially in the morning, when nobody calls. I am no more lonely than the loon in the pond that laughs so loud, or than Walden Pond itself. What company has that lonely lake, I pray? And yet it has not the blue devils, but the blue angels in it, in the azure tint of its waters. God is alone, — but the devil, he is far from being alone; he sees a great deal of company; he is legion.

WALDEN, p. 148.

Sympathy of nature with the human race. The indescribable innocence and beneficence of Nature, — of sun and wind and rain, of summer and winter, — such health, such cheer, they afford forever! and such sympathy have they ever with our race, that all Nature would be affected, and the sun's brightness fade, and the winds would sigh humanely, and the clouds rain tears, and the woods shed their leaves and put on mourning in midsummer, if any man should ever for a just cause grieve. Shall I not have intelligence with the earth? Am I not partly leaves and vegetable mould myself?

WALDEN, p. 149.

Hebe pre-
ferred to
Hygeia.   I am no worshiper of Hygeia, who was the daughter of that old herb - doctor Æsculapius, but rather of Hebe, cupbearer to Jupiter, who was the daughter of Juno and wild lettuce, and who had the power of restoring gods and men to the vigor of youth. She was probably the only thoroughly sound - conditioned, healthy, and robust young lady that ever walked the globe, and wherever she came, it was spring.   WALDEN, p. 150.

Animal food
offends the
imagination.   It is hard to provide and cook so simple and clean a diet as will not offend the imagination ; but this, I think, is to be fed when we feed the body ; they should both sit down at the same table. It may be vain to ask why the imagination will not be reconciled to flesh and fat. I am satisfied that it is not. Whatever my own practice may be, I have no doubt that it is a part of the destiny of the human race, in its gradual improvement, to leave off eating animals, as surely as the savage tribes have left off eating each other when they came in contact with the more civilized.   WALDEN, p. 232.

The slightest intimations of one's genius to be regarded. The faintest assured objection which one healthy man feels will at length prevail over the arguments and customs of mankind. No man ever followed his genius till it misled him. Though the result were bodily weakness, yet perhaps no one can say that the consequences were to be regretted, for these were a life in conformity to higher principles. If the day and the night are such that you greet them with joy, and life emits a fragrance like flowers and sweet-scented herbs, is more elastic, more starry, more immortal, — that is your success. All nature is your congratulation, and you have cause momentarily to bless yourself. The greatest gains and values are farthest from being appreciated. We easily come to doubt if they exist. We soon forget them. They are the highest reality. Perhaps the facts most astounding and most real are never communicated by man to man. The true harvest of my daily life is somewhat as intangible and indescribable as the tints of morning or evening. It is a little star-dust caught, a segment of the rainbow which I have clutched.

WALDEN, p. 233.

Inspiration through the palate. Who has not sometimes derived an inexpressible satisfaction from his food in which appetite had no share ? I have been thrilled to think that I owed a mental perception to the commonly gross sense of taste, that I have been inspired through the palate, that some berries which I had eaten on a hill-side had fed my genius. WALDEN, p. 234.

The quality of the appetite makes the sensualist. He who distinguishes the true savor of his food can never be a glutton ; he who does not cannot be otherwise. A puritan may go to his brown - bread crust with as gross an appetite as ever an alderman to his turtle. Not that food which entereth into the mouth defileth a man, but the appetite with which it is eaten ; it is neither the quantity nor the quality, but the devotion to sensual savors. WALDEN, p. 235.

The moral quality of nature and life. Our whole life is startlingly moral. There is never an instant's truce between virtue and vice. Goodness is the only investment that never fails. In the music of the harp that trembles round the world it is

the insisting on this which thrills us.
Though the youth at last grows indifferent,
the laws of the universe are not indifferent, but are forever on the side of the
most sensitive.   Listen to every zephyr
for some reproof, for it is surely there, and
he is unfortunate who does not hear it.
We cannot touch a string or move a stop
but the charming moral transfixes us.
Many an irksome noise, go a long way off,
is heard as music, a proud sweet satire on
the meanness of our lives.   WALDEN, P. 235.

Delicacy of the distinction between men and beasts.   "That in which men differ from brute beasts," says Mencius, "is a thing very inconsiderable ; the common herd lose it very soon ; superior men preserve it carefully."   WALDEN, P. 236.

Purity inspires the soul.   Chastity is the flowering of man ; and what are called Genius, Heroism, Holiness, and the like, are but various fruits which succeed it.   Man flows at once to God when the channel of purity is open.   By turns our purity inspires and our impurity casts us down.   He is blessed who is assured that the animal is dying out in him day by day, and the divine being established.   WALDEN, P. 236.

Purity and sensuality each a single thing. All sensuality is one, though it takes many forms; all purity is one. It is the same whether a man eat, or drink, or sleep sensually. They are but one appetite, and we only need to see a person do any one of these things to know how great a sensualist he is. The impure can neither stand nor sit with purity. When the reptile is attacked at one mouth of his burrow, he shows himself at another.   WALDEN, p. 237.

Work a help against sin. If you would avoid uncleanness, and all the sins, work earnestly, though it be at cleaning a stable. Nature is hard to be overcome, but she must be overcome.   WALDEN, p. 237.

Every one a sculptor. Every man is the builder of a temple, called his body, to the god he worships, after a style purely his own, nor can he get off by hammering marble instead. We are all sculptors and painters, and our material is our own flesh and blood and bones. Any nobleness begins at once to refine a man's features, any meanness or sensuality to imbrute them.
    WALDEN, p. 238.

The purification of a soul gives it a new life. A voice said to him [John Farmer], — Why do you stay here and live this mean moiling life, when a glorious existence is possible for you? Those same stars twinkle over other fields than these. But how to come out of this condition and actually migrate thither? All he could think of was to practice some new austerity, to let his mind descend into his body and redeem it, and treat himself with ever increasing respect. WALDEN, p. 239.

Strike at the root of social ills by purifying your own life. There are a thousand hacking at the branches of evil to one who is striking at the root, and it may be that he who bestows the largest amount of time and money on the needy is doing the most by his mode of life to produce that misery which he strives in vain to relieve. It is the pious slave-breeder devoting the proceeds of every tenth slave to buy a Sunday's liberty for the rest. Some show their kindness to the poor by employing them in their kitchens. Would they not be kinder if they employed themselves there? WALDEN, p. 82.

Overflowing love the charity which hides a multitude of sins.

I do not value chiefly a man's uprightness and benevolence, which are, as it were, his stem and leaves. Those plants of whose greenness withered we make herb tea for the sick serve but a humble use, and are most employed by quacks. I want the flower and fruit of a man ; that some fragrance be wafted over from him to me, and some ripeness flavor our intercourse. His goodness must not be a partial and transitory act, but a constant superfluity, which costs him nothing and of which he is unconscious. This is a charity that hides a multitude of sins.   WALDEN, p. 83.

What saddens the reformer.

I believe that what so saddens the reformer is not his sympathy with his fellows in distress, but, though he be the holiest son of God, is his private ail. Let this be righted, let the spring come to him, the morning rise over his couch, and he will forsake his generous companions without apology.   WALDEN, p. 84.

Our own cheerful sanity most helpful to others.

All health and success does me good, however far off and withdrawn it may appear ; all disease

and failure helps to make me sad and does
me evil, however much sympathy it may
have with me or I with it.   If, then, we
would restore mankind by truly Indian,
botanic, magnetic, or natural means, let us
be as simple and well as Nature ourselves,
dispel the clouds which hang over our own
brows, and take up a little life into our
pores.   Do not stay to be an overseer of
the poor, but endeavor to become one of
the worthies of the world.   WALDEN, p. 85.

The true
wealth.
A man is rich in proportion to
the number of things which he
can afford to let alone.   WALDEN, p. 89.

The best
crop which
a farm
affords.
With respect to landscapes, —

"I am monarch of all I *survey*,
My right there is none to dispute."

I have frequently seen a poet withdraw,
having enjoyed the most valuable part of a
farm, while the crusty farmer supposed that
he had got a few wild apples only.   Why,
the owner does not know it for many years
when a poet has put his farm in rhyme, the
most admirable kind of invisible fence, —
has fairly impounded it, milked it, skimmed
it, and got all the cream, and left the farmer
only the skimmed milk.   WALDEN, p. 90.

Slavery
to affairs.
As long as possible, live free and uncommitted. It makes but little difference whether you are committed to a farm or the county jail.   WALDEN, p. 91.

Make the
most of what
is good in
life.
I do not propose to write an ode to dejection, but to brag as lustily as chanticleer in the morning standing on his roost, if only to wake my neighbors up.   WALDEN, p. 92.

The creation
a poem to
open ears.
The winds which passed over my dwelling were such as sweep over the ridges of mountains, bearing the broken strains, or celestial parts only, of terrestrial music. The morning wind forever blows, the poem of creation is uninterrupted ; but few are the ears that hear it. Olympus is but the outside of the earth everywhere.   WALDEN, p. 92.

The invita-
tion of morn-
ing.
Every morning was a cheerful invitation to make my life of equal simplicity, and I may say innocence, with Nature herself.   WALDEN, p. 96.

A new life
each day.
They say that characters were engraven on the bathing tub of

king Tching-Thang to this effect: "Renew thyself completely each day; do it again, and again, and forever again."

WALDEN, p. 96.

We should be awakened each morning by new inward life.

Little is to be expected of that day, if it can be called a day, to which we are not awakened by our Genius, but by the mechanical nudgings of some servitor, are not awakened by our own newly acquired force and aspirations from within to a higher life than we fell asleep from.

WALDEN, p. 96.

The organs of one's genius reinvigorated by healthful sleep.

After a partial cessation of his sensuous life, the soul of man, or its organs rather, are reinvigorated each day, and his Genius tries again what noble life it can make.

WALDEN, p. 97.

Morning is whenever we are truly awake.

To him whose elastic and vigorous thought keeps pace with the sun, the day is a perpetual morning. It matters not what the clocks say, or the attitudes and labors of men. Morning is when I am awake and there is a dawn in me.

WALDEN, p. 97.

No one thoroughly awake.   To be awake is to be alive. I have never yet met a man who was quite awake. How could I have looked him in the face?   WALDEN, p. 98.

Expectation of the dawn.   We must learn to reawaken and keep ourselves awake, not by mechanical aids, but by an infinite expectation of the dawn, which does not forsake us in our soundest sleep.   WALDEN, p. 98.

Give beauty to the day from the beauty within.   It is something to be able to paint a particular picture, or to carve a statue, and so to make a few objects beautiful; but it is far more glorious to carve and paint the very atmosphere and medium through which we look, which morally we can do. To affect the quality of the day,—that is the highest of arts.   WALDEN, p. 98.

Real life.   I did not wish to live what was not life, living is so dear; nor did I wish to practice resignation, unless it was quite necessary.   WALDEN, p. 98.

Life not to be lost in the complexity of affairs.   Our life is frittered away by detail.   Simplicity, simplicity, simplicity! Let your affairs be as two or three, and not a hundred or a thousand ; instead of a million count half a dozen, and keep your accounts on your thumb nail. WALDEN, p. 99.

"Plain living and high thinking." The nation itself is just such an unwieldy and overgrown establishment, cluttered with furniture and tripped up by its own traps, ruined by luxury and heedless expense, by want of calculation and a worthy aim, as the million households in the land ; and the only cure for it as for them is in a rigid economy, a stern and more than Spartan simplicity of life and elevation of purpose. WALDEN, p. 99.

Life wasted in affairs. Why should we live with such hurry and waste of life ? We are determined to be starved before we are hungry. Men say that a stitch in time saves nine, and so they take a thousand stitches to-day to save nine to-morrow. WALDEN, p. 100.

The news as compared with eternal truth. What news ! how much more important to know what that is which was never old ! "Kieou-he-yu (great dignitary of the state of Wei) sent a man to Khoung-tseu to know his news. Khoung-Tseu caused the messenger to be seated near him, and questioned him in these terms: 'What is your master doing?' The messenger answered with respect, 'My master desires to diminish the number of his faults, but he cannot come to the end of them.' The messenger being gone, the philosopher remarked: 'What a worthy messenger! What a worthy messenger!'" WALDEN, p. 103.

What alone has reality.   If we respected only what is inevitable and has a right to be, music and poetry would resound along the streets. When we are unhurried and wise, we perceive that only great and worthy things have any permanent and absolute existence, — that petty fears and petty pleasures are but the shadow of the reality. This is always exhilarating and sublime. WALDEN, p. 103.

The great reality is ever here and now.   God himself culminates in the present moment, and will never be more divine in all the ages. And we are enabled to apprehend at all what is sublime and noble, only by the perpetual instilling and drenching of the reality that surrounds us.   WALDEN, p. 105.

Live delib-
erately.   Let us spend one day as deliberately as Nature, and not be thrown off the track by every nutshell and mosquito's wing that falls on the rails. Let us rise early, and fast, or break fast, gently and without perturbation ; let company come and let company go ; let the bells ring and the children cry, — determined to make a day of it.   WALDEN, p. 105.

Seek to
penetrate
through
surfaces to
reality.   Let us settle ourselves, and work and wedge our feet downward through the mud and slush of opinion and prejudice and tradition and delusion and appearance, that alluvion which covers the globe, through Paris and London, through New York and Boston and Concord, through church and state, through poetry and philosophy and religion, till we come to a hard bottom and rocks in place, which we can call *reality*.   WALDEN, p. 105.

Use of the
intellect.   The intellect is a cleaver ; it discerns and rifts its way into the

secret of things. I do not wish to be any
more busy with my hands than is necessary. My head is hands and feet. I feel
all my best faculties concentrated in it.

WALDEN, p. 106.

The shallow
stream of
time.
 Time is but the stream I go
a-fishing in. I drink at it ; but
while I drink, I see the sandy bottom and
detect how shallow it is. Its thin current
slides away, but eternity remains. I would
drink deeper, — fish in the sky, whose bottom is pebbly with stars. WALDEN, p. 106.

Mortality
and im-
mortality.
 In accumulating property for
ourselves or our posterity, in
founding a family or a state, or acquiring
fame even, we are mortal ; but in dealing
with truth we are immortal, and need fear
no change nor accident. WALDEN, p. 108.

How to read
the heroic
books.
 The heroic books, even if
printed in the character of our
mother tongue, will always be in a language
dead to degenerate times ; and we must
laboriously seek the meaning of each word
and line, conjecturing a larger sense than

common use permits, out of what wisdom
and valor and generosity we have.

WALDEN, p. 109.

What are
"the clas-
sics"? Men sometimes speak as if the
study of the classics would at
length make way for more modern and
practical studies ; but the adventurous stu-
dent will always study classics, in whatever
language they may be written, and however
ancient they may be. For what are the
classics but the noblest recorded thoughts
of men ? They are the only oracles which
are not decayed, and there are such answers to the most modern inquiry in them
as Delphi and Dodona never gave.

WALDEN, p. 110.

How true
books
should be
read. To read well, — that is, to read
true books in a true spirit, — is a
noble exercise, and one that will
task the reader more than any exercise
which the customs of the day esteem. It
requires a training such as the athletes
underwent, the steady intention almost of
the whole life to this object. Books must
be read as deliberately and reservedly as
they were written. WALDEN, p. 110.

Living in the present. We should be blessed if we lived in the present always, and took advantage of every accident that befell us, like the grass which confesses the influence of the slightest dew that falls on it; and did not spend our time in atoning for the neglect of past opportunities, which we call doing our duty. We loiter in winter while it is already spring. WALDEN, p. 336.

The influence of Spring. In a pleasant spring morning all men's sins are forgiven. Such a day is a truce to vice. While such a sun holds out to burn, the vilest sinner may return. Through our own recovered innocence we discern the innocence of our neighbors. WALDEN, p. 336.

Wildness. We need the tonic of wildness, — to wade sometimes in marshes where the bittern and the meadow-hen lurk, and hear the booming of the snipe. At the same time that we are earnest to explore and learn all things, we require that all things be mysterious and inexplorable, — that land and sea be infinitely wild. WALDEN, p. 339.

The glory of the realm within. Be a Columbus to whole new continents and worlds within you, opening new channels, not of trade, but of thought. Every man is the lord of a realm beside which the earthly empire of the Czar is but a petty state, a hummock left by the ice. WALDEN, p. 343.

Know thyself. If you would learn to speak all tongues and conform to the customs of all nations, if you would travel farther than all travellers, be naturalized in all climes, and cause the Sphinx to dash her head against a stone, even obey the precept of the old philosopher, and Explore thyself. WALDEN, p. 344.

The universe conforms to our highest ideas. I learned this, at least, by my experiment : that if one advances confidently in the direction of his dreams, and endeavors to live the life which he has imagined, he will meet with a success unimagined in common hours. In proportion as he simplifies his life, the laws of the universe will appear less complex, and solitude will not be solitude, nor poverty poverty, nor weakness weakness. WALDEN, p. 346.

Realize
your dream.   If you have built castles in the air, your work need not be lost; that is where they should be. Now put the foundations under them.   Walden, p. 346.

Extrava-
gance of
expression.   I desire to speak somewhere *without* bounds, — like a man in a waking moment, to men in waking moments; for I am convinced that I cannot exaggerate enough even to lay the foundation of a true expression. Who that has heard a strain of music feared then lest he should speak extravagantly any more forever?   Walden, p. 347.

Indefinite
words may
be most
significant.   The words which express our faith and piety are not definite; yet they are significant and fragrant, like frankincense, to superior natures.   Walden, p. 347.

Step to the
music you
hear.   If a man does not keep pace with his companions, perhaps it is because he hears a different drummer. Let him step to the music which he hears, however measured or far away. It is not important that he should mature as soon as an apple-tree or an oak. Shall he turn his spring into summer?   Walden, p. 348.

Aim ever at the highest. If the condition of things which we were made for is not yet, what were any reality which we can substitute ? We will not be shipwrecked on a vain reality. Shall we with pains erect a heaven of blue glass over ourselves, though when it is done we shall be sure to gaze still at the true ethereal heaven far above, as if the former were not ? WALDEN, p. 349.

Live for that perfection which is eternal. In an imperfect work time is an ingredient, but into a perfect work time does not enter. WALDEN, p. 349.

Why we are commonly in a false position. No face which we can give to a matter will stead us so well at last as the truth. This alone wears well. For the most part, we are not where we are, but in a false position. Through an infirmity of our natures, we suppose a case, and put ourselves into it, and hence are in two cases at the same time, and it is doubly difficult to get out. WALDEN, p. 350.

The simplicity of truth. In sane moments we regard only the facts, the case that is.

Say what you have to say, not what you ought.   Any truth is better than make-believe.   WALDEN, p. 350.

Make the
best of your
own life.   Love your life, poor as it is, — meet it and live it ; do not shun it and call it hard names.   It is not so bad as you are.   It looks poorest when you are richest.   The fault-finder will find faults even in paradise.   WALDEN, p. 350.

Poverty
need not
take from us   You may perhaps have some pleasant, thrilling, glorious hours,
the purest
enjoyments.   even in a poor-house.   The setting sun is reflected from the windows of the alms-house as brighly as from the rich man's abode ; the snow melts before its door as early in the spring.   WALDEN, p. 350.

Dishonesty
worse than
dependence.   Most think they are above being supported by the town ; but it oftener happens that they are not above supporting themselves by dishonest means, which should be more disreputable.
                                  WALDEN, p. 351.

Humility enriches the soul more than culture.

Do not seek so anxiously to be developed, to subject yourself to many influences to be played on ; it is all dissipation. Humility, like darkness, reveals the heavenly lights. The shadows of poverty and meanness gather around us, " and, lo ! creation widens to our view." WALDEN, p. 351.

Wealth does not help in our pursuit of the highest.

We are often reminded that, if there were bestowed on us the wealth of Crœsus, our aims must still be the same, and our means essentially the same. WALDEN, p. 351.

Advantage of poverty.

If you are restricted in your range by poverty, if you cannot buy books and newspapers, for instance, you are but confined to the most significant and vital experiences ; you are compelled to deal with the material which yields the most sugar and the most starch. WALDEN, p. 351.

Money not necessary for the soul.

Superfluous wealth can buy superfluities only. Money is not required to buy one necessary of the soul. WALDEN, p. 352.

A person
irresistible
on his own
path.

I love to weigh, to settle, to gravitate toward that which most strongly and rightfully attracts me ; — not hang by the beam of the scale and try to weigh less, — not suppose a case, but take the case that is ; to travel the only path I can, and that on which no power can resist me.   WALDEN, p. 352.

Fidelity in
work.

Drive a nail home and clinch it so faithfully that you can wake up in the night and think of your work with satisfaction, — a work at which you would not be ashamed to invoke the Muse. So will help you God, and so only.   Every nail driven should be as another rivet in the machine of the universe, you carrying on the work.   WALDEN, p. 353.

Hospitality
in manners,
not in the
"entertain-
ment."

I sat at a table where were rich food and wine in abundance, and I went away hungry from the inhospitable board.   The hospitality was as cold as the ices. . . . The style, the house and grounds and "entertainment," pass for nothing with me.   I called on the king, but he made me wait in his hall, and conducted like a man incapacitated for hospitality.

There was a man in my neighborhood who lived in a hollow tree. His manners were truly regal. I should have done better had I called on him. WALDEN, p. 353.

Work essential to character. How long shall we sit in our porticoes practicing idle and musty virtues, which any work would make impertinent? As if one were to begin the day with long-suffering, and hire a man to hoe his potatoes; and in the afternoon go forth to practice Christian meekness and charity with goodness aforethought! WALDEN, p. 354.

"More day to dawn." Only that day dawns to which we are awake. There is more day to dawn. The sun is but a morning star. WALDEN, p. 357.

The victory of character. Say not that Cæsar was victorious, With toil and strife who stormed the House of Fame; In other sense this youth was glorious, Himself a kingdom wheresoe'er he came. WEEK, p. 276.

The heart is forever inexperienced. WEEK, p. 278.

Friendship a thing outside of human institutions.
There is on the earth no institution which friendship has established ; it is not taught by any religion ; no scripture contains its maxims.

WEEK, p. 280.

Friendship the dream of all.
No word is oftener on the lips of men than " friendship," and indeed no thought is more familiar to their aspirations. All men are dreaming of it, and its drama, which is always a tragedy, is enacted daily. It is the secret of the universe.

WEEK, p. 281.

The actual friend but a suggestion of the ideal.
It is equally impossible to forget our friends, and to make them answer to our ideal. When they say farewell, then indeed we begin to keep them company. How often we find ourselves turning our backs on our actual friends, that we may go and meet their ideal cousins !

WEEK, p. 281.

A friend nourishes the soul.
Even the utmost good will and harmony and practical kindness are not sufficient for friendship, for friends do not live in harmony, merely, as some say, but in melody. We do not wish for

friends to feed and clothe our bodies, —
neighbors are kind enough for that, — but
to do the like office to our spirits. For
this, few are rich enough, however well
disposed they may be. Week, p. 282.

A friend,
the true
educator. Think of the importance of
friendship in the education of
men. It will make a man honest ; it will
make him a hero ; it will make him a saint.
It is the state of the just dealing with the
just, the magnanimous with the magnanimous, the sincere with the sincere, man
with man. Week, p. 283.

The friend
the only radi-
cal reformer. All the abuses which are the
object of reform with the philan-
thropist, the statesman, and the house-
keeper, are unconsciously amended in the
intercourse of friends. Week, p. 283.

It takes two to speak the truth, — one
to speak, and another to hear. Week, p. 283.

Men ask too
seldom to be
nobly dealt
with. In our daily intercourse with
men, our nobler faculties are dor-
mant and suffered to rust. None
will pay us the compliment to expect no-

bleness from us. We ask our neighbor to suffer himself to be dealt with truly, sincerely, nobly; but he answers no by his deafness. He does not even hear this prayer. Week, p. 284.

Society content with a too narrow justice. The state does not demand justice of its members, but thinks that it succeeds very well with the least degree of it, hardly more than rogues practice; and so do the family and the neighborhood. What is commonly called friendship is only a little more honor among rogues. Week, p. 284.

Hearty truth is one with love. Between whom there is hearty truth there is love; and in proportion to our truthfulness and confidence in one another, our lives are divine and miraculous, and answer to our ideal.
Week, p. 284.

The purest love a glimpse of heaven. There are passages of affection in our intercourse with mortal men and women, such as no prophecy had taught us to expect, which transcend our earthly life and anticipate heaven for us. Week, p. 284.

Estrange-
ment.
Between two by nature alike and fitted to sympathize, there is no veil, and there can be no obstacle. Who are the estranged ? Two friends explaining. WINTER, p. 1.

Friends are
not selected.
The books for young people say a great deal about the *selection* of friends ; it is because they really have nothing to say about *friends*. They mean associates and confidants merely. . . . Friendship takes place between those who have an affinity for one another, and is a perfectly natural and inevitable result. No professions nor advances will avail. WEEK, p. 285.

Friends not
anxious to
please each
other.
Impatient and uncertain lovers think that they must say or do something kind whenever they meet ; they must never be cold. But they who are friends do not do what they *think* they must, but what they *must*. Even their friendship is, in one sense, a sublime phenomenon to them. WEEK, p. 285.

Friends help
each other's
loftiest
dreams.
The friend asks no return but that his friend will religiously accept and wear and not disgrace

his apotheosis of him. They cherish each other's hopes. They are kind to each other's dreams.   WEEK, p. 286.

Between friends, good will is necessary, not conscious.

No such affront can be offered to a friend as a conscious good-will, a friendliness which is not a necessity of the friend's nature.

WEEK, p. 286.

Friendship is no respecter of sex; and perhaps it is more rare between the sexes than between two of the same sex.

WEEK, p. 287.

A hero's love is as delicate as a maiden's.

WEEK, p. 287.

My friend is that one whom I can associate with my choicest thought.

WEEK, p. 288.

The toleration of faults an obstacle to friendship.

Beware lest thy friend learn at last to tolerate one frailty of thine, and so an obstacle be raised to the progress of thy love.   WEEK, p. 288.

The purest friendship the most unconscious. Friendship is never established as an understood relation. Do you demand that I be less your friend that you may know it? W**eek**, p. 288.

Genuine invitation. Wait not till I invite thee, but observe that I am glad to see thee when thou comest. .W**eek**, p 289.

Where my friend lives, there are all riches and every attraction, and no slight obstacle can keep me from him. W**eek**, p. 289.

The language of friendship is not words, but meanings. It is an intelligence above language. W**eek**, p. 289.

Friendship requires wisdom as well as tenderness. It is one proof of a man's fitness for friendship that he is able to do without that which is cheap and passionate. A true friendship is as wise as it is tender. W**eek**, p. 290.

Friendship is not conscious kindliness. When the friend comes out of his heathenism and superstition, and breaks his idols, being converted by the precepts of a newer testament ; when he forgets his mythology, and treats his friend like a Christian, or as he can afford, — then friendship ceases to be friendship, and becomes charity ; that principle which established the almshouse is now beginning with its charity at home, and establishing an almshouse and pauper relations there.   WEEK, p. 291.

Friendship is in the interest of humanity.

A base friendship is of a narrowing and exclusive tendency, but a noble one is not exclusive ; its very superfluity and dispersed love is the humanity which sweetens society, and sympathizes with foreign nations ; for, though its foundations are private, it is in effect a public affair and a public advantage, and the friend, more than the father of a family, deserves well of the state.

WEEK, p. 293.

Are any noble enough for a lasting friendship?

The only danger in friendship is that it will end. It is a delicate plant, though a native. The least unworthiness, even if it be unknown to one's self, vitiates it. Let the friend know that those faults which he observes in his friend his own faults attract. . . .

Perhaps there are none charitable, none disinterested, none wise, noble, and heroic enough, for a true and lasting friendship.

Friends do not ask to be appreciated. I sometimes hear my friends complain finely that I do not appreciate their fineness. I shall not tell them whether I do or not. As if they expected a vote of thanks for every fine thing which they uttered or did! Who knows but it was finely appreciated? It may be that your silence was the finer thing of the two.

WEEK, p. 294.

Between friends silence is understood. In human intercourse the tragedy begins, not when there is misunderstanding about words, but when silence is not understood. Then there can never be an explanation.

WEEK, p. 294.

The reserve of affection. We often forbear to confess our feelings, not from pride, but for fear that we could not continue to love the one who required us to give such proof of our affection.

WEEK, p. 295.

A friend cherishes one's highest aspirations. For a companion, I require one who will make an equal demand on me with my own genius. Such a one will always be rightly tolerant. It is suicide and corrupts good manners to welcome any less than this. I value and trust those who love and praise my aspiration rather than my performance. If you would not stop to look at me, but look whither I am looking and farther, then my education could not dispense with your company. WEEK, p. 296.

I cannot leave my sky
    For thy caprice ;
True love would soar as high
    As heaven is.

The eagle would not brook
    Her mate thus won,
Who trained his eye to look
    Beneath the sun.   WEEK, p. 297.

Friendship only between what is highest in each. Confucius said, " To contract ties of friendship with any one, is to contract friendship with his virtue. There ought not to be any other motive in friendship." WEEK, p. 298.

The faults of our friend must be lost in love. It is impossible to say all that we think, even to our truest friend. We may bid him farewell forever sooner than complain, for our complaint is too well grounded to be uttered. WEEK, p. 299.

Friends must be silent about constitutional differences. The constitutional differences which always exist, and are obstacles to a perfect friendship, are forever a forbidden theme to the lips of friends. They advise by their whole behavior. Nothing can reconcile them but love. WEEK, p. 299.

The necessity itself for explanation, — what explanation will atone for that ? WEEK, p. 299.

The real differences between friends cannot be explained away. True love does not quarrel for slight reasons, — such mistakes as mutual acquaintances can explain away ; but, alas, however slight the apparent cause, only for adequate and fatal and everlasting reasons, which can never be set aside. Its quarrel, if there is any, is ever recurring, notwithstanding the beams of affection which invariably come to gild its tears. WEEK, p. 300.

We must accept or refuse one another as we are. I could tame a hyena more easily than my friend.   WEEK, p. 300.

No real life without love. Ignorance and bungling, with love, are better than wisdom and skill without. There may be courtesy, there may be even temper and wit and talent and sparkling conversation, there may be good-will even, and yet the humanest and divinest faculties pine for exercise. Our life without love is like coke and ashes.   WEEK, p. 300.

The inward dawn.

Nature doth have her dawn each
      day,
   But mine are far between;
Content, I cry, for sooth to say,
   Mine brightest are, I ween.

For when my sun doth deign to rise,
   Though it be her noontide,
Her fairest field in shadow lies,
   Nor can my light abide.   WEEK, p. 301.

Friendship and the love of nature harmonize. As I love nature, as I love singing birds, and gleaming stubble, and flowing rivers, and morning

and evening, and summer and winter, I love
thee, my friend. WEEK, p. 302.

The friend
leaves the
sweetest
consolation
at his death.
Even the death of friends will
inspire us as much as their lives.
They will leave consolation to the
mourners, as the rich leave money to de-
fray the expenses of their funerals, and
their memories will be incrusted over with
sublime and pleasing thoughts, as monu-
ments of other men are overgrown with
moss. WEEK, p. 302.

Two solitary stars, —
Unmeasured systems far
Between us roll,
But by our conscious light we are
Determined to one pole. WEEK, p. 304.

Civility
between
friends.
Lying on lower levels is but a
trivial offense compared with civility and compliments on the level of
friendship. WINTER, p. 428.

Exalting
effect of
music.
We are all ordinarily in a state
of desperation. Such is our life,
it ofttimes drives us to suicide. To how

many, perhaps to most, life is barely tolerable ; and if it were not for the fear of death
or of dying, what a multitude would imme-
diately commit suicide ! But let us hear a
strain of music, and we are at once adver-
tised of a life which no man had told us
of, which no preacher preaches.

WINTER, p. 181.

No warder at the gate
Can let the friendly in,
But, like the sun, o'er all
He will the castle win,
And shine along the wall.

WEEK, p. 305.

Implacable is Love :
Foes may be bought or teased
From their hostile intent,
But he goes unappeased
Who is on kindness bent.

WEEK, p. 305.

Simplify
the problem
of life.
When the mathematician would
solve a difficult problem, he first
frees the equation of all encumbrances, and
reduces it to its simplest terms. So simplify the problem of life, distinguish the

necessary and the real.   Probe the earth
to see where your main roots run.

LETTERS, p. 43.

Our faintest
dream points
to the solid-
est reality.
This, our respectable daily life,
in which the man of common
sense, the Englishman of the
world, stands so squarely, and on which
our institutions are founded, is in fact the
veriest illusion, and will vanish like the
baseless fabric of a vision ; but that faint
glimmer of reality which sometimes illu-
minates the darkness of daylight for all
men, reveals something more solid and enduring than adamant, which is in fact the
corner-stone of the world.   LETTERS, p. 44

The realiza-
tion of
dreams.
Men cannot conceive of a state
of things so fair that it cannot
be realized.   LETTERS, p. 44.

We never have a fantasy so subtile and
ethereal, but that *talent merely*, with more
resolution and faithful persistency, after a
thousand failures, might fix and engrave it
in distinct and enduring words, and we
should see that our dreams are the solidest
facts that we know.   LETTERS, p. 45.

What can be expressed in words can be expressed in life.   Letters, p. 45.

We can
respect our
aspirations,
not our
actual lives.
My actual life is a fact, in view of which I have no occasion to congratulate myself; but for my faith and aspiration I have respect.

Letters, p. 45.

I love reform better than its modes. There is no history of how bad became better.   Letters, p. 45.

As for positions, combinations, and details, — what are they? In clear weather, when we look into the heavens, what do we see but the sky and the sun?

Letters, p. 45.

Individual
life the true
source of
reform.
If you would convince a man that he does wrong, do right. But do not care to convince him. Men will believe what they see. Let them see.   Letters, p. 46.

"Do what
you love."
Pursue, keep up with, circle round and round your life, as a dog does his master's chaise. Do what you

love. Know your own bone; gnaw at it, bury it, unearth it, and gnaw it still.

LETTERS, p. 46.

"If ye be led by the spirit, ye are not under the law." Aim above morality. Be not simply good; be good for something. All fables, indeed, have their morals; but the innocent enjoy the story.

LETTERS, p. 46.

Direct appeal to the highest. Let nothing come between you and the light. Respect men as brothers only. When you travel to the Celestial City, carry no letter of introduction. When you knock, ask to see God, — none of the servants.

LETTERS, p. 46.

In what concerns you much, do not think you have companions; know that you are alone in the world.

LETTERS, p. 46.

The true bread. I have tasted but little bread in my life. It has been mere grub and provender for the most part. Of bread that nourished the brain and the heart, scarcely any. There is absolutely none, even on the tables of the rich.

LETTERS, p. 47.

The delight of really earning a living.   Some men go a-hunting, some a-fishing, some a-gaming, some to war; but none have so pleasant a time as they who in earnest seek to earn their bread. It is true actually as it is true really; it is true materially as it is true spiritually, that they who seek honestly and sincerely, with all their hearts and lives and strength, to earn their bread, do earn it, and it is sure to be very sweet to them. LETTERS, p. 48.

A very little bread, — a very few crumbs are enough, if it be of the right quality, for it is infinitely nutritious. Let each man, then, earn at least a crumb of bread for his body before he dies, and know the taste of it, — that it is identical with the bread of life, and that they both go down at one swallow. LETTERS, p. 48.

Not only the rainbow and sunset are beautiful, but to be fed and clothed, sheltered and warmed aright, are equally beautiful and inspiring. There is not necessarily any gross and ugly fact which may not be eradicated from the life of man. LETTERS, p. 49.

The earnest man irresistible. How can any man be weak who dares *to be* at all? Even the tenderest plants force their way up through the hardest earth, and the crevices of rocks; but a man no material power can resist. What a wedge, what a beetle, what a catapult is an *earnest* man! What can resist him? LETTERS, p. 49.

That we have but little faith is not sad, but that we have but little faithfulness. By faithfulness faith is earned. LETTERS, p. 50.

The misery of disobedience to our genius. When once we fall behind ourselves, there is no accounting for the obstacles that rise up in our path, and no one is so wise as to advise, and no one so powerful as to aid us while we abide on that ground. Such are cursed with *duties*, and the *neglect of their duties*. For such the decalogue was made, and other far more voluminous and terrible codes. LETTERS, p. 50.

Cling to the thread of life. Be not anxious to avoid poverty. In this way the wealth of the universe may be securely invested.

What a pity if we do not live this short time according to the laws of the long time, — the eternal laws! . . . In the midst of this labyrinth let us live a *thread* of life.   LETTERS, p. 52.

The laws of earth and heaven harmonize. The laws of earth are for the feet, or inferior man; the laws of heaven are for the head, or superior man; the latter are the former sublimed and expanded, even as radii from the earth's centre go on diverging into space.   LETTERS, p. 53.

Happy the man who observes the heavenly and terrestrial law in just proportion; whose every faculty, from the soles of his feet to the crown of his head, obeys the law of its level; who neither stoops nor goes on tiptoe, but lives a balanced life, acceptable to nature and to God.

LETTERS, p. 53.

Newspapers. If words were invented to conceal thought, I think that newspapers are a great improvement on a bad invention. Do not suffer your life to be taken by newspapers.   LETTERS, p. 56.

Rest for the soul. When we are weary with travel, we lay down our load and rest by the wayside. So, when we are weary with the burden of life, why do we not lay down this load of falsehoods which we have volunteered to sustain, and be refreshed as never mortal was ? Let the beautiful laws prevail. Let us not weary ourselves by resisting them. LETTERS, p. 57.

God most truly found when not consciously sought. It is not when I am going to meet him, but when I am just turning away and leaving him alone, that I discover that God is. I say, God. I am not sure that that is the name. You will know whom I mean. LETTERS, p. 58.

Self renunciation. If for a moment we make way with our petty selves, wish no ill to anything, apprehend no ill, cease to be but as the crystal which reflects a ray, — what shall we not reflect ! What a universe will appear crystallized and radiant around us ! LETTERS, p. 58.

The muse should lead, the understanding follow. The muse should lead like a star which is very far off ; but that does not imply that we are to follow foolishly, falling into sloughs and over precipices, for it is not foolishness, but understanding, which is to follow, which the muse is appointed to lead, as a fit guide of a fit follower.   LETTERS, p. 58.

Too high a demand cannot be made upon life.   Men make a great ado about the folly of demanding too much of life (or of eternity?), and of endeavoring to live according to that demand. It is much ado about nothing. No harm ever came from that quarter.

LETTERS, p. 59.

Danger of undervaluing life.   I am not afraid that I shall exaggerate the value and significance of life, but that I shall not be up to the occasion which it is. I shall be sorry to remember that I was there, but noticed nothing remarkable, — not so much as a prince in disguise; lived in the golden age a hired man; visited Olympus even, but fell asleep after dinner, and did not hear the conversation of the gods.

LETTERS, p. 59.

The kind of news we really want.   We, demanding news, and putting up with *such* news! Is it a new convenience, or a new accident, or, rather, a new perception of the truth that we want ? LETTERS, p. 60.

Divine ex-
pectations. Is not the attitude of expectation somewhat divine ? — a sort of home-made divineness ? Does it not compel a kind of sphere-music to attend on it ? and do not its satisfactions merge at length, by insensible degrees, in the enjoyment of the thing expected ? LETTERS, p. 61.

Exalted em-
ployment. Some absorbing employment on your higher ground, — your upland farm, — whither no cart-path leads, but where you mount alone with your hoe, — where the life everlasting grows ; there you raise a crop which needs not to be brought down into the valley to a market ; which you barter for heavenly products.

LETTERS, p. 61.

Yield not to
melancholy
in the up-
ward path. Be not deterred by melancholy on the path which leads to immortal health and joy. When they tasted of the water of the river over which they were to go, they thought it tasted a little bitterish to the palate, but it proved sweeter when it was down. LETTERS, p. 62.

As a man thinketh, so is he.   Our thoughts are the epochs in our lives; all else is but as a journal of the winds that blew while we were here.   LETTERS, p. 63.

Our ideal shames our best efforts.   It is not easy to make our lives respectable by any course of activity.   We must repeatedly withdraw into our shells of thought, like the tortoise, somewhat helplessly; yet there is more than philosophy in that.   LETTERS, p. 64.

Inward poverty.   If I should turn myself inside out, my rags and meanness would indeed appear.   I am something to him that made me, undoubtedly, but not much to any other that he has made.

LETTERS, p. 64.

He who obeys his genius cannot lose his friends.   As for missing friends, — what if we do miss one another? Have we not agreed on a rendezvous? While each wanders his own way through the wood, without anxiety, ay, with serene joy, though it be on his hands and knees, over rocks and fallen trees, he cannot but be in the right way.   There is no wrong way to him.   LETTERS, p. 65.

Friendship in nature. A man who missed his friend at a turn, went on buoyantly, dividing the friendly air, and humming a tune to himself, ever and anon kneeling with delight to study each lichen in his path, and scarcely made three miles a day for friendship. LETTERS, p. 65.

Unconscious influence. I am glad to know that I am as much to any mortal as a persistent and consistent scarecrow is to a farmer, — such a bundle of straw in a man's clothing as I am, with a few bits of tin to sparkle in the sun dangling about me, as if I were hard at work there in the field. However, if this kind of life saves any man's corn, — why, he is the gainer. LETTERS, p. 68.

The best appreciation is discriminating. I am not afraid you will flatter me as long as you know what I am, as well as what I think or aim to be, and distinguish between these two; for then it will commonly happen that if you praise the last, you will condemn the first. LETTERS, p. 69.

All the world complain now-a-days of a press of trivial duties and engagements, which prevents their employing themselves on some higher ground they know of ; but undoubtedly, if they were made of the right stuff to work on that higher ground, provided they were released from all those engagements, they would now at once fulfill the superior engagement, and neglect all the rest, as narurally as they breathe.   LETTERS, p. 70.

The earnest not hindered by trifles.

As for passing *through* any great and glorious experience, and rising *above* it, as an eagle might fly athwart the evening sky to rise into still brighter and fairer regions of the heavens, I cannot say that I ever sailed so creditably, but my bark ever seemed thwarted by some side wind, and went off over the edge, and now only occasionally tacks back toward the centre of that sea again.   LETTERS, p. 70.

A glorious experience cannot be left behind.

I have outgrown nothing good, but, I do not fear to say, fallen behind by whole continents of virtue, which should have been passed as islands in my

Hope for ourselves.

course ; but I trust — what else can I trust ?
— that with a stiff wind, some Friday, when
I have thrown some of my cargo over-
board, I may make up for all that distance
lost.   LETTERS, p. 71.

Wisdom and love essential to each other.
Man is continually saying to
woman, Why will you not be
more wise ? Woman is continually saying to man, Why will you not be
more loving ? It is not in their wills to be
wise or to be loving ; but, unless each is
both wise and loving, there can be neither
wisdom nor love.   LETTERS, p. 72.

Sky-lights.
I am not satisfied with ordinary
windows. I must have a true sky-light,
and that is outside the village. . . . The
man I meet with is not often so instructive
as the silence he breaks. This stillness,
solitude, wildness of nature is a kind of
thoroughwort or boneset to my intellect.
This is what I go out to seek. It is as if
I always met in those places some grand,
serene, immortal, infinitely encouraging,
though invisible, companion, and walked
with him. There at last my nerves are
steadied, my senses and my mind do their
office.   WINTER, p. 135.

The human
eye.   The lover sees in the glance of his beloved the same beauty that in the sunset paints the western skies. It is the same *daimōn* here lurking under a human eyelid and there under the closing eyelids of the day. Here, in small compass, is the ancient and natural beauty of evening and morning. What loving astronomer has ever fathomed the ethereal depths of the eye ?   LETTERS, p. 73.

The lover's
reserve.   Perhaps an instinct survives through the intensest actual love, which prevents entire abandonment of devotion, and makes the most ardent lover a little reserved. It is the anticipation of change. For the most ardent lover is not the less practically wise, and seeks a love which will last forever.   LETTERS, p. 73.

The rarity
of real
marriages.   Considering how few poetical friendships there are, it is remarkable that so many are married. It would seem as if men yielded too easy an obedience to nature without consulting their genius. One may be drunk with love without being any nearer to finding his mate.   LETTERS, p. 74.

Both common and divine sense should be consulted in marriage.

If common sense had been consulted, how many marriages would never have taken place; if uncommon or divine sense, how few marriages, such as we witness, would ever have taken place! LETTERS, p. 74.

Love should be ascending.

Our love may be ascending or descending. What is its character, if it may be said of it, —

> " We must *respect* the souls above,
> But only those below we *love*."

LETTERS, p. 74.

Shun a descending love.

Is your friend such a one that an increase of worth on your part will rarely make her more your friend? Is she retained, — is she attracted, — by more nobleness in you, — by more of that virtue which is peculiarly yours; or is she indifferent and blind to that? Is she to be flattered and won by your meeting her on any other than the ascending path? Then duty requires that you separate from her.

LETTERS, p. 74.

True love most clear-sighted.

A man of fine perceptions is more truly feminine than a merely

sentimental woman. The heart is blind ;
but love is not blind. None of the gods is
so discriminating.   LETTERS, p. 75.

In love. the
imagination
must not be
offended.

In love and friendship the imagination is as much exercised as
the heart ; and if either is out-
raged, the other will be estranged.   It
is commonly the imagination which is
wounded first, rather than the heart, — it
is so much the more sensitive.

LETTERS, p. 75.

Lovers must
understand
each another
without
words.

I require that thou knowest
everything without being told
anything.   I parted from my beloved because there was one thing which I
had to tell her.   She *questioned* me.   She
should have known all by sympathy.   That
I had to tell it her was the difference between us, — the misunderstanding.

LETTERS, p. 76.

The lover
hears things,
not words.

A lover never hears anything
that is *told*, for that is commonly
either false or stale ; but he hears things
taking place, as the sentinels heard Trenck

mining in the ground, and thought it was
moles.   LETTERS, p. 76.

Love de-   If to chaffer and higgle are
mands the
utmost di-   bad in trade, they are much worse
rectness.
             in love. It demands directness
as of an arrow.   LETTERS, p. 77.

The true   The lover wants no partiality.
lover would
not hide his He says, Be so kind as to be just.
faults.
             . . . I need thy hate as much as
thy love. Thou wilt not repel me entirely
when thou repellest what is evil in me.
                                          LETTERS, p. 77.

Truthfulness. It is not enough that we are
truthful; we must cherish and carry out
high purposes to be truthful about.
                                          LETTERS, p. 78.

No lower en-   Commonly, men are as much
gagement can
stand in the   afraid of love as of hate. They
way of love.   have lower engagements. They
have near ends to serve. They have not
imagination enough to be thus employed
about a human being, but must be cooper-
ing a barrel, forsooth.   LETTERS, p. 78.

No treasure to be compared with love.

What a difference whether, in all your walks, you meet only strangers, or in one house is one who knows you, and whom you know. To have a brother or a sister! To have a gold mine on your farm! To find diamonds in the gravel heaps before your door! How rare these things are!   LETTERS, p. 78.

"Through thee alone the sky is arched.
Through thee the rose is red."

Would not a friend enhance the beauty of the landscape as much as a deer or a hare? Everything would acknowledge and serve such a relation; the corn in the field, and the cranberries in the meadow. The flowers would bloom and the birds sing with a new impulse. There would be more fair days in the year.   LETTERS, p. 78.

"On the earth the broken arcs, in the heaven a perfect sound."

The object of love expands and grows before us to eternity, until it includes all that is lovely, and we become all that can love.

LETTERS, p. 79.

Meet others on the highest plane you can command.

If you seek the warmth even of affection from a similar motive to that from which cats and

dogs and slothful persons hug the fire, because your temperature is low through
sloth, you are on the downward road, and
it is but to plunge yet deeper into sloth.

LETTERS, p. 81.

Genuine
love elevates
and
strengthens.
The warmth of celestial love
does not relax, but nerves and
braces its enjoyer. Warm your
body by healthful exercise, not by cower-
ing over a stove. Warm your spirit by
performing independently noble deeds, not
by ignobly seeking the sympathy of your
fellows who are no better than yourself.

LETTERS, p. 81.

Friends deal
in pure
truth with
each other.
A man's social and spiritual
discipline must answer to his cor-
poreal. He must lean on a friend
who has a hard breast, as he would lie on
a hard bed. He must drink cold water for
his only beverage. So he must not hear
sweetened and colored words, but pure and
refreshing truths. He must daily bathe in
truth cold as spring water, not warmed by
the sympathy of friends. LETTERS, p. 81.

We must love our friend so much that

she shall be associated with our purest and holiest thoughts alone. When there is impurity, we have "descended to meet," though we knew it not.   LETTERS, p. 82.

Love must be vigilant to retain its purity. We may love and not elevate one another. The love that takes us as it finds us degrades us. What watch we must keep over the fairest and purest of our affections, lest there be some taint about them. May we so love as never to have occasion to repent our love.   LETTERS, p. 82.

A flower the symbol of pure love. Flowers, which, by their infinite hues and fragrance, celebrate the marriage of the plants, are intended for a symbol of the open and unsuspected beauty of all true marriage, when man's flowering season arrives.   LETTERS, p. 82.

The joy of love and of intellectual perception. A true marriage will differ in no wise from illumination. In all perception of the truth there is a divine ecstasy, an inexpressible delirium of joy, as when a youth embraces his betrothed virgin. The ultimate delights of a true marriage are one with this.

LETTERS, p. 84.

Pure love the radical reformer. Some have asked if the stock of men could not be improved,— if they could not be bred as cattle. Let love be purified, and all the rest will follow. A pure love is thus, indeed, the panacea for all the ills of the world. LETTERS, p. 84.

The offspring of the noble tend to a higher nobility. The only excuse for reproduction is improvement. Nature abhors repetition. Beasts merely propagate their kind; but the offspring of noble men and women will be superior to themselves, as their aspirations are. By their fruits ye shall know them.

LETTERS, p. 84.

Faithfulness rather than knowledge saves the soul. As to how to preserve potatoes from rotting my opinion may change from year to year; but as to how to preserve my soul from rotting, I have nothing to learn, but something to practice. LETTERS, p. 87.

Wealth complicates the problem of life. The problem of life becomes, one cannot say by how many degrees, more complicated as our material wealth is increased, whether that needle they tell of was a gateway or not, since the problem is not merely nor mainly to get life for our bodies, but by this or a similar discipline to get life for our souls; by cultivating the lowland farm on right principles, that is, with this view, to turn it into an upland farm.   LETTERS, p. 88.

To truly earn our bread, we must satisfy God for it.   Though we are desirous to earn our bread, we need not be anxious to *satisfy* men for it, — though we shall take care to pay them, — but God, who alone gave it to us.   LETTERS, p. 89.

Men may punish us for satisfying God.   Men may in effect put us in the debtors' jail for that matter, simply for paying our whole debt to God, which includes our debt to them, and though we have his receipt for it, for his paper is dishonored.   LETTERS, p. 90.

How prompt we are to satisfy the hunger and thirst of our bodies; how slow to satisfy the hunger and thirst of our *souls.*

LETTERS, p. 90.

Care for the body compared with care for the soul.   An ordinary man will work every day for a year at shovelling dirt to support his body, or a family of bodies ; but he is an extraordinary man who will work a whole day in a year for the support of his soul. LETTERS, p. 90.

Real success. He alone is the truly enterprising and practical man who succeeds in *maintaining* his soul here. Have we not our everlasting life to get ? and is not that the only excuse for eating, drinking, sleeping, or even carrying an umbrella when it rains ? LETTERS, p. 90.

The helpful friend encourages our aspirations. I am much indebted to you because you look so steadily at the better side, or rather the true centre of me (for our true centre may, and perhaps oftenest does, lie entirely aside from us, and we are in fact eccentric), and, as I have elsewhere said, "give me an opportunity to live." LETTERS, p. 91.

The ideal needs but slight support in the actual. What a little shelf is required, by which we may impinge upon another, and build there our eyrie in the clouds, and all the heavens we see above us we refer to the crags around and beneath us. Some piece of mica, as it were, in the face or eyes of one, as on the delectable mountains, slanted at the right angle, reflects the heavens to us.

LETTERS, p. 91.

How the ideal transfigures a person.   It was not the hero I admired, but the reflection from his epaulet or helmet.   It is nothing (for us) permanently inherent in another, but his attitude or relation to what we prize, that we admire.   The meanest man may glitter with micaceous particles to his fellow's eye.   These are the spangles that adorn a man.   LETTERS, p. 91.

Ideal union.   The highest union, . . . or central oneness, is the coincidence of visual rays. Our club-room was an apartment in a constellation where our visual rays met (and there was no debate about the restaurant). The way between us is over the mount.

LETTERS, p 92.

Yourself and myself lost in the highest union.   Your words make me think of a man of my acquaintance whom I occasionally meet, whom you, too, appear to have met, one Myself, as he is called.   Yet, why not call him *Yourself*?   If you have met with him and know him, it is all I have done ; and surely where there is mutual acquaintance, the *my* and *thy* make a distinction without a difference.   LETTERS, p. 92.

The most indefinite thought significant.   Hold fast to your most indefinite, waking dream. The very green dust on the walls is an organized vegetable ; the atmosphere has its fauna and flora floating in it ; and shall we think that dreams are but dust and ashes, are always disintegrated and crumbling thoughts, and not dust-like thoughts trooping to their standard with music, systems beginning to be organized ?   LETTERS, p. 92.

Value of a clear soul compared with material gains.   Suppose a man were to sell the hue, the least amount of coloring matter in the superficies of his thought, for a farm,—were to exchange an absolute and infinite value for a relative and finite one, to gain the whole world and lose his own soul !   LETTERS, p. 93.

Self-respect.   It is worth while to live respectably unto ourselves. We can possibly *get along* with a neighbor, even with a bedfellow, whom we respect but very little ; but as soon as it comes to that, that we do not respect ourselves, then we do not get along at all, no matter how much money we are paid for halting.   LETTERS, p. 95.

Better obscurity above than false clearness below.

It is better to have your head in the clouds, and know where you are, if indeed you cannot get it above them, than to breathe the clearer atmosphere below them, and think that you are in paradise.   LETTERS, p. 96.

Appeal to the highest within you.

All that men have said or are is a very faint rumor, and it is not worth while to remember or refer to that. If you are to meet God, will you refer to anybody out of that court? How shall men know how I succeed, unless they are in at the life? I did not see the "Times" reporter there.   LETTERS, p. 96.

Friends must meet erectly.

We will stand on solid foundations to one another,—I a column planted on this shore, you on that. . . . We will not mutually fall over that we may meet, but will grandly and eternally guard the straits.   LETTERS, p. 119.

The comfort of industry.   Talk of burning your smoke after the wood has been consumed! There is a far more important and warming heat, commonly lost, which precedes the burning of the wood. It is the smoke of industry, which is incense. I had been so thoroughly warmed in body and spirit, that when at length my fuel was housed, I came near selling it to the ashman, as if I had extracted all its heat.

LETTERS, p. 128.

Providing necessaries, not superfluities, a pleasure.   Is it not delightful to provide one's self with the necessaries of life, — to collect dry wood for the fire when the weather grows cool, or fruits when we grow hungry? — not till then. And then we have all the time left for thought!   LETTERS, p. 96.

A warm body and a cold spirit.   Of what use were it, pray, to get a little wood to burn to warm your body this cold weather, if there were not a divine fire kindled at the same time to warm your spirit?   LETTERS, p. 97.

The true dawn.   Life is so short that it is not wise to take roundabout ways, nor can we spend much time in waiting. Is it absolutely necessary, then, that we should do as we are doing ? . . . Though it is late to leave off this wrong way, it will seem early the moment we begin in the right way ; instead of mid-afternoon, it will be early morning with us. We have not got half-way to dawn yet.   LETTERS, p. 97.

Necessity of work. We must heap up a great pile of doing for a small diameter of being. Is it not imperative on us that we *do* something, if we only work in a tread-mill ? And, indeed, some sort of revolving is necessary to produce a centre and nucleus of being. What exercise is to the body, employment is to the mind and morals.   LETTERS, p. 99.

Unconsciousness of beauty. There are so many layers of mere white lime in every shell to that thin inner one so beautifully tinted. Let not the shell-fish think to build his house of that alone ; and pray, what are its tints to him ? Is it not his smooth, close-fitting shirt merely, whose tints *are not* to him, being in the dark, but only when he is gone or dead, and his shell is heaved up

to light, a wreck upon the beach, do they
appear.   LETTERS, p. 99.

High results How admirably the artist is
of work. made to accomplish his self-cul-
ture by devotion to his art! The wood-
sawyer, through his effort to do his work
well, becomes not merely a better wood-
sawyer, but measurably a better *man*.

LETTERS, p. 100.

No dilettan- You say that you do not suc-
teism. ceed much. Does it concern you
enough that you do not? Do you work
hard enough at it? Do you get the bene-
fit of discipline out of it? If so, persevere.
Is it a more serious thing than to walk a
thousand miles in a thousand successive
hours? Do you get any corns by it? Do
you ever think of hanging yourself on account of failure?   LETTERS, p. 100.

It is the art of mankind to polish the
world, and every one who works is scrub-
bing in some part.   LETTERS, p. 101.

The higher If the work is high and far, you
the aim, the
more earnest must not only aim aright, but
must be the
work. draw the bow with all your might.

You must qualify yourself to use a bow which no humbler archer can bend.

" Work, — work, — work ! "

Who shall know it for a bow ? It is not of yew-tree. It is straighter than a ray of light ; flexibility is not known for one of its qualities.   LETTERS, p. 101.

Work in spite of moods. Whether a man spends his day in an ecstasy or despondency, he must do some work to show for it, even as there are flesh and bones to show for him. We are superior to the joy we experience.

LETTERS, p. 103.

The loneliness of false society. Ah ! what foreign countries there are, greater in extent than the United States or Russia, and with no more souls to a square mile, stretching away on every side from every human being, with whom you have no sympathy. . . . Rocks, earth, brute beasts, comparatively, are not so strange to me.

LETTERS, p. 105.

When I sit in the parlors and kitchens of some with whom my business brings me — I was going to say in contact — (busi-

ness, like misery, makes strange bedfel-
lows), I feel a sort of awe, and as forlorn as
if I were cast away on a desolate shore.   I
think of Riley's narrative and his suf-
ferings. LETTERS, p. 105.

How finite   You, who soared like a merlin
unlikeness
isolates   with your mate through the realms
souls.   of ether, in the presence of the
unlike drop at once to earth, a mere amor-
phous squab, divested of your air-inflated
pinions. . . . You travel on, however,
through this dark and desert world; you
see in the distance an intelligent and sym-
pathizing lineament; stars come forth in
the dark, and oases appear in the desert.
LETTERS, p. 105.

The friend   I am glad to hear that I do not
does not
limit our   always limit your vision when you
vision.   look this way; that you sometimes see the light through me ; that I am
here and there windows, and not all dead
wall.   Might not the community sometimes
petition a man to remove himself as a
nuisance, a darkener of the day, a too
large mote? LETTERS, p. 107.

Humanity before Nature. The best news you send me is, not that Nature with you is so fair and genial, but that there is one there who likes her so well. That proves all that was asserted. Letters, p. 111.

Things correspond to our highest idea. I have not yet learned to live, that I can see, and I fear that I shall not very soon. I find, however, that in the long run things correspond to my original idea, — that they correspond to nothing else so much. Letters, p. 113.

Courage. When an Indian is burned, his body may be broiled, it may be no more than a beefsteak. What of that? They may broil his *heart*, — but they do not therefore broil his *courage*, — his principles. Be of good courage! That is the main thing. Letters, p. 113.

To the courageous all burdens become light. If a man were to place himself in an attitude to bear manfully the greatest evil that can be inflicted on him, he would find suddenly that there was no such evil to bear; his brave back would go a-begging. . . . But as long as he crouches, and skulks, and shirks his work, every creature that has weight will be treading on his toes, and crushing him; he will himself tread with one foot on the other foot.   LETTERS, p. 114.

The dreadful thing not outside of us. The monster is never just there where we think he is. What is truly monstrous is our cowardice and sloth.

LETTERS, p. 114.

The true adviser. Why should we ever go abroad, even across the way, to ask a neighbor's advice? There is a nearer neighbor within us incessantly telling us how we should behave. But we wait for the neighbor without to tell us of some false, easier way.   LETTERS, p. 114.

Fatal post-ponement. In every one of these houses there is at least one man fighting or squabbling a good part of his time with a dozen pet demons of his own breeding and cherishing, which are relentlessly gnawing at his vitals; and if perchance he resolve at length that he will courageously combat them, he says, "Ay! Ay! I will attend to you after dinner." And, when that time comes, he concludes that he is good for another stage, and reads a column or two about the *Eastern War!*   LETTERS, p. 115.

We must account for our lives.   At last one will say, " Let us see, how much wood did you burn, sir ?" and I shall shudder to think that the next question will be, " What did you do while you were warm ?" Do we think the ashes will pay for it ? that God is an ashman ? It is a fact that we have got to render an account for the deeds done in the body.   LETTERS, p. 115.

Sincerity is a great but rare virtue, and we pardon to it much complaining, and the betrayal of many weaknesses.   LETTERS, p. 117.

Simplicity of life not an end, but a means.   To what end do I lead a simple life at all, pray ? That I may teach others to simplify their lives ? — and so all our lives be *simplified* merely, like an algebraic formula ? Or not, rather, that I may make use of the ground I have cleared, to live more worthily and profitably ?   LETTERS, p. 117.

I would fain lay the most stress forever

on that which is the most important, — imports the most to me, — though it were only (what it is likely to be) a vibration in the air. LETTERS, p. 118.

The mountains within us.   I was glad to hear the other day that Higginson and Brown were gone to Ktaadn ; it must be so much better to go to than a Woman's Rights or Abolition Convention ; better still, to the delectable, primitive mounts within you, which you have dreamed of from your youth up, and seen, perhaps, in the horizon, but never climbed.

LETTERS, p. 118.

Poverty of nature and internal wealth.   A walk over the crust to Asnybumskit, standing there in its inviting simplicity, is tempting to think of, — making a fire on the snow under some rock ! The very poverty of outward nature implies an inward wealth in the walker. What a Golconda is he conversant with, thawing his fingers over such a blaze ! LETTERS, p. 137.

Helpful society.   As for the dispute about solitude and society, any comparison is impertinent. It is an idling down on the plain at the base of a mountain, instead of climbing steadily to its top. Of course you will be glad of all the society you can get to go up with. Will you go to glory with me? is the burden of the song. LETTERS. p. 139.

It is not that we love to be alone, but that we love to soar, and when we do soar, the company grows thinner and thinner till there is none at all. It is either the tribune on the plain, a sermon on the mount, or a very private ecstasy still higher up. We are not the less to aim at the summits, though the multitude does not ascend them. Use all the society that will abet you.   LETTERS, p. 139.

Gratitude for the sense of existence.   I am grateful for what I am and have. My thanksgiving is perpetual. It is surprising how contented one can be with nothing definite, — only a sense of existence.   LETTERS, p. 145.

The doubleness of our lives.   Methinks a certain polygamy with its troubles is the fate of almost all men. They are married to two wives, their genius (a celestial muse), and also to some fair daughter of the earth. Unless these two were fast friends before marriage, and so are afterward, there will be but little peace in the house.

LETTERS, p. 154.

Our deeper
convictions
unchange-
able

It is a great satisfaction to find that your oldest convictions are permanent. With regard to essentials I have never had occasion to change my mind. . . . The aspect of the world varies from year to year, as the landscape is differently clothed, but I find that the truth is still true, and I never regret any emphasis it may have inspired. Ktaadn is there still, but much more surely my conviction is there, resting with more than mountain breadth and weight on the world, the source still of fertilizing streams, and affording glorious views from its summit if I can get up to it again. *LETTERS, p. 137.*

Style in
writing.

As for style of writing, if one has anything to say, it drops from him simply and directly, as a stone falls to the ground. There are no two ways about it, but down it comes, and he may stick in the points and stops wherever he can get a chance. . . . To try to polish the stone in its descent, to give it a peculiar turn, and make it whistle a tune, perchance would be of no use, if it were possible.   LETTERS, p. 158.

Appetite for solitude.   As some heads cannot carry much wine, so it would seem that I cannot bear so much society as you can. I have an immense appetite for solitude, like an infant for sleep, and if I don't get enough of it this year, I shall cry all the next.   LETTERS, p. 160.

An adventure in the mind rather than in the thing done.   If you have been to the top of Mount Washington, let me ask, What did you find there?   That is the way they prove witnesses, you know. Going up there and being blown on is nothing.   We never do much climbing while we are there, but we eat our luncheon, etc., very much as at home.   It is after we get home that we really go over the mountain, if ever.   What did the mountain say? What did the mountain do?   LETTERS, p. 165.

Be warmed by activity.   Now is the time to become conversant with your wood-pile (this comes under Work for the Month), and be sure you put some warmth into it by your way of getting it. Do not consent to be passively warmed. An intense degree of that is the hotness that is threatened. But a positive warmth within can withstand the fiery furnace, as the vital heat of a living man can withstand the heat that cooks meat. Letters, p. 167.

Friends found in solitude. I have lately got back to that glorious society, called Solitude, where we meet our friends continually, and can imagine the outside world also to be peopled. Yet some of my acquaintances would fain hustle me into the almshouse for *the sake of society*, as if I were pining for that diet, when I seem to myself a most befriended man, and find constant employment. Letters, p. 173.

What a fool he must be who thinks that his El Dorado is anywhere but where he lives. Letters, p. 177.

The battle in behalf of sane think-ing. What a battle a man must fight everywhere to maintain his stand-ing army of thoughts, and march with them in orderly array through the

always hostile country ! How many ene-
mies there are to sane thinking. Every
soldier has succumbed to them before he
enlists for those other battles.

LETTERS, p. 179.

The cost of
hospitality
to our best
thoughts.
It is easy enough to maintain a
family, or a state, but it is hard
to maintain these children of your
brain (or say, rather, these guests that trust
to enjoy your hospitality), they make such
great demands ; and yet, he who does only
the former, and loses the power to *think*
originally, or as only he ever can, fails mis-
erably. Keep up the fires of thought, and
all will go well. LETTERS, p. 180.

Real success
or failure
is in our
thoughts.
How you can overrun a country, climb any rampart, and carry
any fortress, with an army of
alert thoughts ! — thoughts that send their
bullets home to heaven's door, — with
which you can *take* the whole world, without paying for it, or robbing anybody. See,
the conquering hero comes ! You *fail* in
your thoughts, or you *prevail* in your
thoughts only. LETTERS, p. 180.

Thought a
solvent for
the world.
In your mind must be a liquor which will dissolve the world whenever it is dropt in it. There is no universal solvent but this, and all things together cannot saturate it. It will hold the universe in solution, and yet be as translucent as ever.   LETTERS, p. 181.

Right think-
ing irresist-
ible.
Provided you *think* well, the heavens falling, or the earth gaping, will be music for you to march by. No foe can ever see you, or you him; you cannot so much as *think* of him; swords have no edges, bullets no penetration, for such a contest.   LETTERS, p. 180.

The beauty
or misery of
life, in our
thoughts.
Look at mankind. No great difference between two, apparently; perhaps the same height, and breadth, and weight; and yet, to the man who sits most east, this life is a weariness, routine, dust and ashes, and he drowns his imaginary *cares* (!) (a sort of friction among his vital organs) in a bowl. But to the man who sits most west, his *contemporary* (!), it is a field for all noble endeavors, an elysium, the dwelling-place of heroes and demigods. The former complains that

he has a thousand affairs to attend to ; but
he does not realize that his affairs (though
they may be a thousand) and he are one.

LETTERS, p. 182.

Grade the ground before you build. What is the use of a house if
you have n't got a tolerable pla-
net to put it on ? — if you cannot
tolerate the planet it is on? Grade the
ground first.   LETTERS, p. 183.

A man's Elysium or Tophet in himself. If a man believes and expects
great things of himself, it makes
no odds where you put him, or
what you show him (of course *you* cannot
put him anywhere, nor show him anything),
he will be surrounded by grandeur. He
is in the condition of a healthy and hungry
man, who says to himself, How sweet
this crust is ! If he despairs of himself,
then Tophet is his dwelling-place, and he
is in the condition of a sick man who is
disgusted with the fruits of finest flavor.

LETTERS, p. 183.

Whether he sleeps or wakes, — whether
he runs or walks, — whether he uses a
microscope or a telescope, or his naked

eye, — a man never discovers anything, never overtakes anything, or leaves anything behind, but himself. Whatever he says or does, he merely reports himself.

LETTERS, p. 183.

Courage. Each reaching and aspiration is an instinct with which all nature consists and coöperates, and therefore it is not in vain. But alas! each relaxation and desperation is an instinct too. To be active, well, happy, implies rare courage.

LETTERS, p. 184.

Success comes from devotion to ideas. The fact is, you have got to take the world on your shoulders like Atlas, and put along with it. You will do this for an idea's sake, and your success will be in proportion to your devotion to ideas. It may make your back ache occasionally, but you will have the satisfaction of hanging it or twirling it to suit yourself. Cowards suffer, heroes enjoy. After a long day's walk with it, pitch it into a hollow place, sit down and eat your luncheon. Unexpectedly, by some immortal thoughts, you will be compensated. The bank whereon you sit will be a fragrant and flowery one, and your world in the hollow, a sleek and light gazelle.

LETTERS, p. 184.

Explore the Unknown by mending your ways. What is the use of going right over the old track again ? There is an adder in the path which your own feet have worn. You must make tracks into the Unknown. That is what you have your board and clothes for. Why do you ever mend your clothes, unless that, wearing them, you may mend your ways.

LETTERS, p. 185.

One's proper work, and dissipation. I am very busy, after my fashion, little as there is to show for it, and feel as if I could not spend many days nor dollars in traveling ; for the shortest visit must have a fair margin to it, and the days thus affect the weeks, you know. Nevertheless, we cannot forego these luxuries altogether. LETTERS, p. 187.

The shallowness of complaint. This life is not for complaint, but for satisfaction. . . . Any complaint *I* have to make is too serious to be uttered, for the evil cannot be mended.

LETTERS, p. 188.

Unconscious goodness.   How wholesome winter is, seen far or near; how good, above all mere sentimental, warm-blooded, short-lived, soft-hearted, *moral* goodness, commonly so-called. Give me the goodness which has forgotten its own deeds, — which God has seen to be good, and let be. LETTERS, p. 194.

What business have you, if you are "an angel of light," to be pondering over the deeds of darkness, reading the "New York Herald" and the like? LETTERS, p. 195.

I will not doubt the love untold
Which not my worth nor want hath bought,
Which wooed me young, and woos me
     old,
And to this evening hath me brought.

LETTERS, p. 219.

The ideal of a walk.   Every walk is a sort of crusade, preached by some Peter the Hermit in us, to go forth and reconquer this Holy Land from the hands of the Infidels.

EXCURSIONS, p. 162.

A true walker made so by the grace of God.   No wealth can buy the requisite leisure, freedom, and independence, which are the capital in this profession. It comes only by the grace of God. It requires a direct dispensation from Heaven to become a walker.

EXCURSIONS, p. 163.

True walking is not for exercise.   The walking of which I speak has nothing in it akin to taking exercise, as it is called, as the sick take medicine at stated hours, — as the swinging of dumb-bells or chairs; but is itself the enterprise and adventure of the day. If you would get exercise, go in search of the springs of life. Think of a man's swinging dumb-bells for his health, when those springs are bubbling up in far-off pastures unsought by him. EXCURSIONS, p. 166.

Worldly cares forgotten in a true walk.   In my walks I would fain return to my senses. What business have I in the woods, if I am thinking of something out of the woods? I suspect myself, and cannot help a shudder, when I find myself so implicated even in what are called good works, — for this may sometimes happen.

EXCURSIONS, p. 169.

The interest of a new prospect. An absolutely new prospect is a great happiness, and I can get this any afternoon. . . . A single farmhouse which I had not seen before is sometimes as good as the dominions of the King of Dahomey. EXCURSIONS, p. 169.

Nature prevails over man in a large landscape. From many a hill I can see civilization and the abodes of man afar. The farmers and their works are scarcely more obvious than wood-chucks and their burrows. Man and his affairs, church and state and school, trade and commerce, and manufactures and agriculture, even politics, the most alarming of them all, — I am pleased to see how little space they occupy in the landscape. EXCURSIONS, p. 170.

To enjoy a thing exclusively is commonly to exclude yourself from the true enjoyment of it. EXCURSIONS, p. 175.

The charm of wildness. There are some intervals which border the strain of the woodthrush, to which I would migrate, — wild lands where no settler has squatted, to to which, methinks, I am already acclimated. EXCURSIONS, p. 186.

The most alive, the wildest. Life consists with wildness. The most alive is the wildest. Not yet subdued to man, its presence refreshes him. One who pressed forward incessantly and never rested from his labors, who grew fast and made infinite demands on life, would always find himself in a new country or wilderness, and surrounded by the raw material of life.   EXCURSIONS, p. 187.

The attractiveness of swamps. I derive more of my subsistence from the swamps which surround my native town than from the cultivated gardens in the village. There are no richer pastures to my eyes than the dense beds of dwarf andromeda which cover these tender places on the earth's surface.   EXCURSIONS, p. 188.

My spirits infallibly rise in proportion to the outward dreariness. Give me the ocean, the desert, or the wilderness.

EXCURSIONS, p. 189.

Wild thinking delights us. It is the uncivilized, free, and wild thinking in "Hamlet" and the "Iliad," in all the Scriptures and Mythologies, not learned in the schools, that delights us.   EXCURSIONS, p. 193.

Wildness of the best books.   A truly good book is something as natural and as unexpectedly and unaccountably fair and perfect as a wild flower discovered on the prairies of the West or in the jungles of the East. Excursions, p. 193.

No poetry so wild as Nature.   I do not know of any poetry to quote which adequately expresses this yearning for the Wild. Approached from this side, the best poetry is tame. I do not know where to find in any literature, ancient or modern, any account which contents me of that Nature with which even I am acquainted.   Excursions, p. 195.

The soul above science.   By long years of patient industry and reading of the newspapers, — for what are the libraries of science but files of newspapers? — a man accumulates a myriad facts, lays them up in his memory, and then when in some spring of his life he scampers abroad into the Great Fields of thought, he, as it were, goes to grass like a horse, and leaves all his harness behind in the stable.   Excursions, p. 203.

Knowledge sometimes worse than ignorance.   A man's ignorance sometimes is not only useful, but beautiful, — while his knowledge, so called, is oftentimes worse than useless, besides being ugly. Which is the best man to deal with, — he who knows nothing about a subject, and, what is extremely rare, knows that he knows nothing, or he who really knows something about it, but thinks that he knows all?   Excursions, p. 204.

Aim above knowledge.   My desire for knowledge is intermittent; but my desire to bathe my head in atmospheres unknown to my feet is perennial and constant. The highest that we can attain to is not Knowledge, but Sympathy with Intelligence.

Excursions, p. 204.

Free and loving activity, the highest.   "That is active duty," says the Vishnu Purana, "which is not for our bondage; that is knowledge which is for our liberation; all other duty is good only unto weariness; all other knowledge is only the cleverness of an artist."   Excursions, p. 205.

A border life between Nature and Society.   For my part, I feel that with regard to Nature I live a sort of border life, on the confines of a world into which I make occasional and transient forays only, and my patriotism and allegiance to the State into whose territories I seem to retreat are those of a moss-trooper.   EXCURSIONS, p. 207.

Vision through the works of man to the wildness of nature.

The walker in the familiar fields which stretch around my native town sometimes finds himself in another land than is described in their owners' deeds. . . . These farms . . . have no chemistry to fix them; they fade from the surface of the glass, and the picture which the painter painted stands out dimly from beneath.   EXCURSIONS, p. 207.

The realm of thought laid waste by worldly living.

We are accustomed to say in New England that few and fewer pigeons visit us every year. Our forests furnish no mast for them. So, it would seem, few and fewer thoughts visit each growing man from year to year, for the grove in our minds is laid waste, — sold to feed unnecessary fires of ambition, or sent to mill, and there is scarcely a twig left for them to perch on.   EXCURSIONS, p. 209.

The great hope that gives value to life.

So we saunter toward the Holy Land, till one day the sun shall shine more brightly than ever he

has done, shall perchance shine into our
minds and hearts, and light up our whole
lives with a great awakening light, as warm
and serene and golden as on a bank-side in
autumn.   Excursions, p. 214.

The compli-   The greatest compliment that
ment of valu-
ing one's   was ever paid me was when one
thought.
           asked me what *I thought*, and at-
tended to my answer.   I am surprised as
well as delighted when this happens, it is
such a rare use he would make of me, as if
he were acquainted with the tool.

                    Yankee in Canada, etc., p. 248.

The glory of   This world is a place of busi-
leisure.
           ness.   What an infinite bustle!
I am awaked almost every night by the
panting of the locomotive.   It interrupts
my dreams.   There is no sabbath.   It
would be glorious to see mankind at leisure
for once.   Yankee in Canada, etc., p. 249.

Out-door   We must go out and re-ally our-
life.
           selves to Nature every day.   We
must make root, send out some little fibre
at least, even every winter day.   I am sensible that I am imbibing health when I

open my mouth to the wind. Staying in the house breeds a sort of insanity always. Every house is, in this sense, a sort of hospital. A night and a forenoon is as much confinement to those wards as I can stand. I am aware that I recover some sanity which I had lost, almost the instant that I come abroad. WINTER, p. 57.

The evil of earning money *merely.* To have done anything by which you earned money *merely* is to have been truly idle or worse. If the laborer gets no more than the wages which his employer pays him, he is cheated; he cheats himself.

YANKEE IN CANADA, ETC., p. 251.

"Work for work's sake." The aim of the laborer should be, not to get his living, to get "a good job," but to perform well a certain work. . . . Do not hire a man who does your work for money, but him who does it for love of it. YANKEE IN CANADA, ETC., p. 252.

The truly efficient man. The community has no bribe that will tempt a wise man. You may raise money enough to tunnel a mountain, but you cannot raise money enough to hire a man who is minding *his own* business. An efficient and valuable man does what he can, whether the community pay him for it or not.

Yankee in Canada, etc., p. 253.

Artificial wants en-slave us.   Perhaps I am more than usually jealous with respect to my freedom. . . . If my wants should be much increased, the labor required to supply them would become a drudgery. If I should sell both my forenoons and afternoons to society, as most appear to do, I am sure that for me there would be nothing left worth living for. I trust that I shall never thus sell my birthright for a mess of pottage.

Yankee in Canada, etc., p. 253.

The constant elevation of our aim.   As for the comparative demand which men make on life, it is an important difference between two, that one is satisfied with a level success, that his marks can all be hit by point-blank shots, but the other, however low and unsuccessful his life may be, constantly elevates his aim, though at a very slight angle to the horizon.   Yankee in Canada, etc., p. 254.

Living and getting a living should be alike beautiful. It is remarkable that there is little or nothing to be remembered written on the subject of getting a living : how to make getting a living not merely honest and honorable, but altogether inviting and glorious ; for if *getting* a living is not so, then living is not.

YANKEE IN CANADA, ETC., p. 254.

Cold and hunger seem more friendly to my nature than those methods which men have adopted and advise to ward them off.

YANKEE IN CANADA, ETC., p. 255.

The ordinary modes of getting a living hostile to true life. The ways in which most men get their living, that is, live, are mere make-shifts, and a shirking of the real business of life, chiefly because they do not know, but partly because they do not mean, any better.

YANKEE IN CANADA, ETC., p. 255.

A grain of gold will gild a great surface, but not so much as a grain of wisdom.

YANKEE IN CANADA, ETC., p. 257.

Where alone the true gold is to be found. Men rush to California and Australia, as if the true gold were to be found in that direction ; but

that is to go to the very opposite extreme
to where it lies. . . . Is not our *native* soil
auriferous? Does not a stream from the
golden mountains flow through our native
valley? and has not this for more than
geologic ages been bringing down the
shining particles and forming the nuggets
for us?   Yankee in Canada, etc., p. 258.

What shall it   A man had better starve at once
profit a man   than lose his innocence in the
if he shall
gain the   process of getting his bread.   If
whole world,
etc.   within the sophisticated man there
is not an unsophisticated one, then he is
but one of the Devil's angels.   As we grow
old we live more coarsely, we relax a little
in our disciplines, and, to some extent, cease
to obey our finest instincts.   But we should
be fastidious to the extreme of sanity, dis-
regarding the gibes of those who are more
unfortunate than ourselves.

                 Yankee in Canada, etc., p. 260.

The limited   I hardly know an *intellectual*
views of
men.   man, even, who is so broad and
truly liberal that you can think aloud in his
society. Most with whom you endeavor
to talk soon come to a stand against some

institution in which they appear to hold stock, — that is, some particular, not universal, way of viewing things. They will continually thrust their own low roof, with its narrow skylight, between you and the sky, when it is the unobstructed heavens you would view.

Yankee in Canada, etc., p. 261.

Religion without the language of religion.

In some lyceums they tell me that they have voted to exclude the subject of religion. But how do I know what their religion is, and when I am near to it or far from it? I have walked into such an arena and done my best to make a clean breast of what religion I have experienced, and the audience never suspected what I was about.

Yankee in Canada, etc., p. 261.

The low demand we make upon each other.

I often accuse my finest acquaintances of an immense frivolity; for, while there are manners and compliments we do not meet, we do not teach one another the lessons of honesty and sincerity that the brutes do, or of steadiness and solidity that the rocks do. The fault is commonly mutual, however ; for we do not habitually demand any more of each other.

YANKEE IN CANADA, ETC., p. 262.

Shallow intercourse. When our life ceases to be inward and private, conversation degenerates into mere gossip. We rarely meet a man who can tell us any news which he has not read in a newspaper, or been told by his neighbor; and, for the most part, the only difference between us and our fellow is, that he has seen the newspaper, or been out to tea, and we have not.

YANKEE IN CANADA, ETC., p. 263.

Life sacrificed to the newspaper. I do not know but it is too much to read one newspaper a week. I have tried it recently, and for so long it seems to me that I have not dwelt in my native region. The sun, the clouds, the snow, the trees say not so much to me. You cannot serve two masters. It requires more than a day's devotion to know and to possess the wealth of a day.

YANKEE IN CANADA, ETC., p. 263.

A world outside that of the newspaper. If you chance to live and move and have your being in that thin stratum in which the events that make the news transpire,— thinner than the paper on which it is printed, — then these things will fill the world for you ; but if you soar above or dive below that plane, you cannot remember nor be reminded of them. YANKEE IN CANADA, ETC., p. 264.

The mind
not to be
desecrated
by gossip
and affairs.
I am astonished to observe how willing men are . . . to permit idle rumors and incidents of the most insignificant kind to intrude on ground which should be sacred to thought. Shall the mind be a public arena, where the affairs of the street and the gossip of the tea-table chiefly are discussed? Or shall it be a quarter of heaven itself, — an hypæthral temple, consecrated to the service of the gods? YANKEE IN CANADA, ETC., p. 265.

Intellectual
and moral
suicide.
It is important to preserve the mind's chastity. . . . Think of admitting the details of a single case of the criminal court into our thoughts, to stalk profanely through their very *sanctum sanctorum* for an hour, ay, for many hours! to make a very bar-room of the mind's inmost apartment, as if for so long the very dust of the street had occupied us, — the

very street itself, with all its travel, its
bustle, and filth, had passed through our
thoughts' shrine! Would it not be an intellectual and moral suicide?

YANKEE IN CANADA, ETC., p. 265.

Let your
mind be
open to the
best.
If I am to be a thoroughfare, I
prefer that it be of the mountain
brooks, Parnassian streams, and
not the town sewers. There is inspiration,
that gossip which comes to the ear of the
attentive mind from the courts of heaven.
There is the profane and stale revelation
of the bar-room and the police court. The
same ear is fitted to receive both communications. Only the character of the hear-
er determines to which it shall be opened,
and to which closed.

YANKEE IN CANADA, ETC., p. 266.

Science
should be
allied to in-
spiration.
Even the facts of science may
dust the mind by their dryness,
unless they are in a sense effaced
each morning, or rather rendered fertile by
the dews of fresh and living truth. Knowledge does not come to us by details, but
in flashes of light from heaven.

YANKEE IN CANADA, ETC., p. 267.

Political freedom but a means. Do we call this the land of the free? . . . What is the value of any political freedom but as a means to moral freedom? . . . It is our children's children who may perchance be really free.

YANKEE IN CANADA, ETC., p. 268.

We quarter our gross bodies on our poor souls, till the former eat up all the latter's substance. YANKEE IN CANADA, ETC., p. 268.

Manners apart from character. It is the vice . . . of manners that they are continually being deserted by the character; they are cast-off clothes or shells, claiming the respect which belonged to the living creature. . . . The man who thrusts his manners upon me does as if he were to insist on introducing me to his cabinet of curiosities when I wished to see himself. It was not in this sense that the poet Decker called Christ "the first true gentleman that ever breathed." YANKEE IN CANADA, ETC., p. 269.

The most precious productions of a state. The chief want, in every State that I have been into, was a high and earnest purpose in its inhabitants. . . . When we want culture more

than potatoes, and illumination more than
sugar-plums, then the great resources of a
world are taxed and drawn out, and the
result, or staple production, is, not slaves,
nor operatives, but men, — those rare fruits
called heroes, saints, poets, philosophers,
and redeemers. Yankee in Canada, etc., p. 271.

Truth and   As a snow-drift is formed where
institutions.   there is a lull in the wind, so, one
would say, where there is a lull of truth, an
institution springs up.   But the truth blows
right on over it, nevertheless, and at length
blows it down.   Yankee in Canada, etc., p. 271.

The author-   Poetry is so universally true
ship of
poetry.   and independent of experience
that it does not need any particular biography to illustrate it, but we refer it sooner
or later to some Orpheus or Linus, and
after ages to the genius of humanity, and
the gods themselves.   Week, p. 102.

Hours above   We should be at the helm at
time.   least once a day.   The whole of
the day should not be daytime ; there
should be one hour, if not more, when the
day did not bring forth.   Week, p. 103.

Read the best books first, or you may not have a chance to read them at all.

WEEK, p. 103.

The hiberna-
tion of the
poet.
The poet is he that hath fat enough, like bears and marmots, to suck his claws all winter. He hibernates in this world, and feeds on his own marrow, . . . is . . . a sort of dormouse gone into winter quarters of deep and serene thoughts, insensible to surrounding circumstances ; his words are the relation of his oldest and finest memory, a wisdom drawn from the remotest experience. Other men lead a starved existence, meanwhile, like hawks that would fain keep on the wing and trust to pick up a sparrow now and then.   WEEK, p. 106.

The rarity of
perfect ex-
pression.
A perfectly healthy sentence is . . . extremely rare. For the most part we miss the hue and fragrance of the thought ; as if we could be satisfied with the dews of morning or evening without their colors, or the heavens without their azure.   WEEK, p. 110.

How phys-
ical labor
may help
the writer.
We are often struck by the force and precision of style to which hard-working men, unpractised in writing, easily attain, when required to make the effort; as if plainness and vigor and sincerity, the ornaments of style, were better learned on the farm and in the workshop than in the schools.

WEEK, p. 113.

Hours of
resolution.
Some hours seem not to be occasion for any deed, but for resolves to draw breath in. We do not directly go about the execution of the purpose that thrills us, but shut our doors behind us and ramble with prepared mind, as if the half were already done. Our resolution is taking root or hold . . . then, as seeds first send a shoot downward, which is fed by their own albumen, ere they send one upward to the light. WEEK, p. 115.

Few speak
simply
enough of
Nature.
The scholar is not apt to make his most familiar experience come gracefully to the aid of his expression. Very few men can speak of Nature, for instance, with any truth. They overstep her modesty somehow or other,

and confer no favor. They do not speak a good word for her. . . . The surliness with which the woodchopper speaks of his woods, handling them indifferently as his axe, is better than the mealy-mouthed enthusiasm of the lover of nature. Better that the primrose by the river's brim be a yellow primrose and nothing more, than that it be something less. WEEK, p. 115.

Always room for a true book. A good book will never have been forestalled, but the topic itself will in one sense be new, and its author, by consulting with Nature, will consult not only with those who have gone before, but with those who may come after. There is always room and occasion enough for a true book on any subject, as there is room for more light the brightest day, and more rays will not interfere with the first. WEEK, p. 116.

Good and bad sleep. One sailor was visited in his dreams this night by the Evil Destinies, and all those powers that are hostile to human life, which constrain and oppress the minds of men, and make their path seem difficult and narrow, and beset

with dangers. . . . But the other hap-
pily passed a serene and even ambrosial
or immortal night, and his sleep was dream-
less, or only the atmosphere of pleasant
dreams remained, — a happy, natural sleep
until the morning, — and his cheerful spirit
soothed and reassured his brother, for
whenever they meet, the Good Genius is
sure to prevail.   WEEK, p. 123.

The signifi-   When we are in health, all
cance of
music.   sounds fife and drum for us; we
hear the notes of music in the air, or catch
its echoes dying away when we awake in
the dawn.   Marching is when the pulse of
the hero beats in unison with the pulse
of Nature, and he steps to the measure of
the universe; then there is true courage
and invincible strength.   WEEK, p. 185.

Music is the sound of the universal laws
promulgated.   It is the only assured tone.
There are in it such strains as far surpass
any man's faith in the loftiness of his destiny.   WEEK, p. 185.

History not   We should read history as little
to be read
critically.   critically as we consider the land-

scape, and be more interested by the at-
mospheric tints and various lights and
shades which the intervening spaces cre-
ate, than by its groundwork and composi-
tion. It is the morning now turned evening and seen in the west, — the same sun,
but a new light and atmosphere. . . . In
reality, history fluctuates as the face of the
landscape from morning to evening. What
is of moment is its hue and color . . .; we
want not its *then*, but its *now*. We do not
complain that the mountains in the horizon
are blue and indistinct; they are the more
like the heavens. WEEK, p. 164.

Divine
leisure.
What are threescore years and
ten, hurriedly and coarsely lived,
to moments of divine leisure, in which your
life is coincident with the life of the universe? We live too fast and coarsely, just
as we eat too fast, and do not know the
true savor of our food. We consult our
will and our understanding and the expectation of men, not our genius. I can im-
pose upon myself tasks which will crush
me for life and prevent all expansion, and
this I am but too inclined to do.
WINTER, p. 45.

The muse
too plaintive. The loftiest strains of the muse are, for the most part, sublimely plaintive, and not a carol as free as nature's. The contest which the sun shines to celebrate from morning to evening is unsung. The muse solaces herself, and is not ravished, but consoled. . . . But in Homer and Chaucer there is more of the serenity and innocence of youth than in the more modern and moral poets.

WEEK, p. 389.

A spontane-
ous inno-
cence above
virtue. To the innocent there are neither cherubims nor angels. At rare intervals we rise above the necessity of virtue into an unchangeable morning light, in which we have only to live right on and breathe the ambrosial air. WEEK, p. 390.

There is no wisdom that can take place of humanity. WEEK, p. 391.

Each deed
determined
by the whole
life. Our whole life is taxed for the least thing well done. It is its net result. How we eat, drink, sleep, and use our desultory hours now in these indifferent days, with no eye to ob-

serve and no occasion to excite us, determines our authority and capacity for the
time to come. Early Spring, p. 22.

A friend's
advice.
A friend advises by his whole
behavior, and never condescends
to particulars. Another chides away a
fault, he loves it away. While he sees the
other's error, he is silently conscious of it,
and only the more loves truth itself, and
assists his friend in loving it, till the fault
is expelled and gently extinguished.

Early Spring, p. 28.

A lesson
from the
flowers.
Simplicity is the law of nature
for men as well as for flowers. •
When the tapestry (corolla) of the nuptial
bed (calyx) is excessive, luxuriant, it is un-
productive. . . . Such a flower has no true
progeny, and can only be reproduced by
the humble mode of cuttings from its stem
or roots. . . . The fertile flowers are single,
not double. Early Spring, p. 28.

The source
of thought
above our-
selves.
I have thoughts, as I walk, on
some subject that is running in
my head, but all their pertinence
seems gone before I can get home to set

them down. The most valuable thoughts which I entertain are anything but what *I* thought. Nature abhors a vacuum, and if I can only walk with sufficient carelessness I am sure to be filled. EARLY SPRING, p. 34.

There must be good hearing to make a good reader. There can be no good reading unless there is good hearing also. It takes two, at least, for this game, as for love, and they must coöperate. EARLY SPRING, p. 52.

An advantage of ignorance. The birds I heard [to-day], which, fortunately, did not come within the scope of my science, sang as freshly as if it had been the first morning of creation, and had for background to their song an untrodden wilderness stretching through many a Carolina and Mexico of the soul. EARLY SPRING, p. 55.

The standard within us. We forget to strive and aspire, to do better even than is expected of us. I cannot stay to be congratulated. I would leave the world behind me. . . . To please our friends and relatives we turn out our silver ore in cartloads, while we neglect to work our mines of gold known only to ourselves, far up in the Sierras, where we pulled up a bush in our mountain walk, and saw the glittering treasure. Let us return thither. Let it be the price of our freedom to make that known.

WINTER, p. 169.

Unconscious reproof. We reprove each other unconsciously by our own behavior. Our very carriage and demeanor in the streets should be a reprimand that will go to the conscience of every beholder. An infusion of love from a great soul gives a color to our faults which will discover them as lunar caustic detects impurities in water. The best will not seem to go contrary to others ; but as if they could afford to travel the same way, they go a parallel but higher course. Jonson says, —

" That to the vulgar canst thyself apply,
Treading a better path, not contrary."

EARLY SPRING, p. 56.

We must love our friend as we love God. How can our love increase unless our loveliness increases also? We must securely love each other as we love God, with no more danger that our love be unrequited or ill bestowed. There is that in my friend before which I must first decay and prove untrue.

EARLY SPRING, p. 62.

Respect your impulses. Impulse is, after all, the best linguist ; its logic, if not conformable to Aristotle, cannot fail to be most convincing. The nearer we can approach to a complete but simple transcript of our thought, the more tolerable will be the piece, for we can endure to consider ourselves in a state of passivity or in involuntary action, but rarely can we endure to consider our efforts, and least of all, our rare efforts. EARLY SPRING, p. 77.

Essential life not to be probed. We must not expect to probe with our fingers the sanctuary of any life, whether animal or vegetable. If we do, we shall discover nothing but surface still. The ultimate expression or fruit of any created thing is a fine effluence, which only the most ingenuous worshiper perceives at a reverent distance from its surface even. . . . Only that intellect makes any progress toward conceiving of the essence which at the same time perceives the effluence. EARLY SPRING, p. 83.

No ripeness merely the means. There is no ripeness which is not, so to speak, something ultimate in itself, and not merely a perfected means to a higher end. In order to be ripe it must serve a transcendent use. The ripeness of a leaf, being perfected, leaves the tree at that point, and never returns to it. EARLY SPRING, p. 84.

Music has no history. A history of music would be like the history of the future, for so little past is it and capable of record that it is but the hint of a prophecy. . . . It has no history more than God. . . . Properly speaking, there can be no history but natural history, for there is no past in the soul, but in nature. . . . I might as well write the history of my aspirations.

EARLY SPRING, p. 85.

The warble of the blue-bird. The bluebird on the apple-tree, warbling so innocently, to inquire if any of its mates are within call, — the angel of the spring! Fair and innocent, yet the offspring of the earth. The color of the sky, *above*, and of the subsoil, *beneath*, suggesting what sweet and innocent melody, terrestrial melody, may have its birthplace between the sky and the ground.

EARLY SPRING, p. 110.

Content-
ment with
the life as-
signed us.
We can only live healthily the life the gods assign us.   I must receive my life as passively as the willow leaf that flutters over the brook.   I must not be for myself, but God's work, and that is always good. . . . My fate cannot but be grand so.   We may live the life of a plant or an animal without living an animal life.   This constant and universal content of the animal comes of resting quietly in God's palm.   EARLY SPRING, p. 111.

The delight
of inter-
course with
a friend.
My friend! my friend! . . . To address thee delights me, there is such clearness in the delivery. I am delivered of my tale, which, told to strangers, still would linger in my life as if untold, or doubtful how it ran.

EARLY SPRING, p. 112.

Real wealth.   I wish so to live ever as to derive my satisfactions and inspirations from the commonest events, every-day phenomena, so that what my senses hourly perceive in my daily walk, the conversations of my neighbors, may inspire me, and I may dream of no heaven but that which lies about me. . . . I do not wish my native soil to become exhausted and run out through neglect. Only that traveling is good which reveals to me the value of home, and enables me to enjoy it better. That man is the richest whose pleasures are the cheapest.

EARLY SPRING, p. 114.

Solitude and society. Mrs. A. takes on dolefully on account of the solitude in which she lives; but she gets little consolation. Mrs. B. says she envies her that retirement. Mrs. A. is aware that she does, and says it is as if a thirsty man should envy another the river in which he is drowning. So goes the world. It is either this extreme or that. Of solitude, one gets too much; another, not enough.

EARLY SPRING, p. 116.

Turn towards the light. The scholar finds in his experience some studies to be most fertile and radiant with light, others, dry, barren, and dark. If he is wise he will not persevere in the last, as a plant in a cellar will strive towards the light. . . . Dwell as near as possible to the channel in which your life flows. A man may associate with such companions, he may pursue such em-

ployments, as will darken the day for him.
Men choose darkness rather than light.

EARLY SPRING, p. 121.

The solitude of a human soul.   How alone must our life be lived.   We dwell on the seashore, and none between us and the sea.   Men are my merry companions, my fellow-pilgrims, who beguile the way, but leave me at the first turn in the road, for none are traveling one road so far as myself. . . . Parents and relatives but entertain the youth.   They cannot stand between him and his destiny.   EARLY SPRING, p. 128.

"The kingdom of God cometh not with observation."   I am startled that God can make me so rich, even with my own cheap stores.   It needs but a few wisps of straw in the sun, some small word dropped, or that has long lain silent in some book.   When heaven begins, and the dead arise, no trumpet is blown.   Perhaps the south wind will blow.   EARLY SPRING, p. 129.

Let love rest on common aspirations.   As soon as I see people loving what they see merely, and not their own high hopes that they form of others, I pity them and do not want their love.

Did I ask thee to love me who hate myself? No! Love that which I love, and I will love thee that loves it. <small>EARLY SPRING, p. 133.</small>

The promise in the face of nature. Life is grand, and so are its environments of Past and Future. Would the face of nature be so serene and beautiful if man's destiny were not equally so? <small>EARLY SPRING, p. 133.</small>

Singleness of purpose. What am I good for now, who am still searching after high things, but to hear and tell the news, to bring wood and water, and count how many eggs the hens lay? In the meanwhile I expect my life to begin. I will not aspire longer. I will see what it is I would be after. I will be unanimous.

<small>EARLY SPRING, p. 134.</small>

Water in early spring. No sooner has the ice of Walden melted than the wind begins to play in dark ripples over the face of the virgin water. It is affecting to see nature so tender, however old, and wearing none of the wrinkles of age. Ice dissolved is the next moment as perfect water as if it had been melted a million years. To see that which was lately so hard and immovable now so soft and impressible! What if our moods could dissolve thus completely? It is like a flush of life on a cheek that was dead. It seems as if it must rejoice in its own newly-acquired fluidity, as it affects the beholder with joy. EARLY SPRING, p. 135.

The privacy of religion. Our religion is as unpublic and incommunicable as our poetical vein, and to be approached with as much love and tenderness. EARLY SPRING, p. 137.

No book can match nature. As I am going to the woods, I think to take some small book in my pocket, whose author has been there already, whose pages will be as good as my thoughts, and will eke them out, or show me human life still gleaming in the horizon when the woods have shut out the town. But I can find none. None will sail as far forward into the bay of nature as my thought. They stay at home. I would go home. When I get to the wood, their thin leaves rustle in my fingers. They are bare and obvious, and there is no halo or haze about them. Nature lies fair and far behind them all, EARLY SPRING, p. 137.

The divinity of the human eye. When God made man he reserved some parts and some rights to himself. The eye has many qualities which belong to God more than man. It is his lightning which flashes therein. When I look into my companion's eye, I think it is God's private mine. It is a noble feature ; it cannot be degraded. For God can look on all things undefiled.

EARLY SPRING, p. 138.

No truth without love. The only way to speak the truth is to speak lovingly. Only the lover's words are heard. The intellect should never speak. It does not utter a natural sound. EARLY SPRING, p. 139.

Disinterested love. The great and solitary heart will love alone, without the knowledge of its object. It cannot have society in its love. It will expend its love as the cloud drops rain upon the fields over which it floats. EARLY SPRING, p. 139.

Aspirations in the spring. I pray that the life of this spring and summer may ever lie fair in my memory. May I dare as I have never done. May I persevere as I have never done. May I purify myself anew as with fire and water, soul and body. May my melody not be wanting to the season. May I gird myself to be a hunter of the beautiful, that naught escape me. May I attain to a youth never attained.

 EARLY SPRING, p. 140.

Human and divine law.   Men make an arbitrary code, and, because it is not right, they try to make it prevail by might. The moral law does not want any champion. Its assertors do not go to war. It was never infringed with impunity. It is inconsistent to deny war and maintain law, for if there were no need of war, there would be no need of law.   EARLY SPRING, p. 147.

The bluebird's note at the end of winter.   How much more habitable a few birds make the fields! At the end of the winter, when the fields are bare, and there is nothing to relieve the monotony of withered vegetation, our life seems reduced to its lowest terms. But let a bluebird come and warble over them, and what a change! The note of the first bluebird in the air answers to the purling rill of melted snow beneath. It is evidently soft and soothing, and, as surely as the thermometer, indicates a higher temperature. It is the accent of the south wind, its vernacular. EARLY SPRING, p. 168.

Nature on the side of what is best in us. Each new year is a surprise to us. We find that we had virtually forgotten the note of each bird, and when we hear it again it is remembered like a dream, reminding us of a previous state of existence. How happens it that the associations it awakens are always pleasing, never saddening, reminiscences of our sanest hours. The voice of nature is always encouraging.

EARLY SPRING, p. 170.

A CONTRIBUTION

TOWARD A

BIBLIOGRAPHY OF THOREAU

"A truth-speaker he, capable of the most deep and strict conversation; a physician to the wounds of any soul." — EMERSON.

PREFACE.

—◆—

"It is the bibliographer who of all men
has most occasion to realize the imperfection of human endeavor.   Completeness in
bibliography is an *ignis fatuus* that eludes
even the closest pursuit and the most pains-
taking endeavor."   If such an adept as Mr.
R. R. Bowker makes the above avowal (and
it may be found in his preface to the
"American Catalogue," 1885), that fact must
plead for the "imperfection" of this bit of
'prentice work, which has been done in
such moments as could be stolen from the
imperative duties of an arduous profession.
To be suddenly summoned from searching
a catalogue to soothe a colic may be "business;" it is hardly bibliographing.

This "Contribution" is not the result of
an "endeavor" at "completeness."   It is

simply a thank-offering to Thoreau's memory, from one who has been "lifted up and
strengthened" by his example.   It was
compiled in the hope that it might facili-
tate the study of, and enlarge an acquaintance with, the author of "the only book
yet written in America, to my thinking,
that bears an annual perusal."   Standing
at Thoreau's graveside some twenty-eight
years ago, Emerson said, — "The country
knows not yet, or in least part, how great
a son it has lost. . . . His soul was made
for the noblest society ; he had in a short
life exhausted the capabilities of this world ;
wherever there is knowledge, wherever
there is virtue, wherever there is beauty, he
will find a home."   There is too much of
truth in the fear that the man so certified
"great, intelligent, sensual, avaricious
America" *knows not yet, or in least part.*
There is peril for the soul in such ignorance.

   To those unacquainted with Thoreau,
this "Contribution" will afford an aid for
which the compiler would long since have

been very grateful. Whatever of worth it may have as a contribution is wholly due to courtesies received from H. S. Salt, London; Geo. Willis Cooke; Wm. C. Lane, Harvard College Library; R. C. Davis, Librarian of the University of Michigan; to whom be thanks.

Ann Arbor, 24*th May*, 1890.

A CONTRIBUTION TOWARD A BIBLIOGRAPHY

OF

HENRY DAVID THOREAU.

———◆———

I.

PAPERS, POEMS, AND BOOKS BY THOREAU.

1840. Sympathy. *The Dial*, i. 71 (July). Reprinted in the collection of poems at the close of *Letters to Various Persons*.

Aulus Persius Flaccus. *The Dial*, i. 117 (July). Reprinted in *A Week on the Concord and Merrimack Rivers*, p. 326.

1841. Stanzas: "Nature doth have her dawn each day." *The Dial*, i. 314 (January). Reprinted in *A Week on the Concord and Merrimack Rivers*, p. 301.

Sic Vita. *The Dial*, ii. 81 (July). Reprinted in *A Week on the Concord and Merrimack Rivers*, p. 405.

Friendship. *The Dial*, ii. 204 (October). Reprinted under the title, "Romans, Countrymen, and Lovers," in the collection of poems at the close of *Letters to Various Persons;* also in *A Week on the Concord and Merrimack Rivers*, p. 304.

1842. Natural History of Massachusetts. *The Dial,* iii. 19 (July). Reprinted in *Excursions.*

Prayers. *The Dial,* iii. 77 (July). Reprinted in *A Yankee in Canada, with Anti-Slavery and Reform Papers.*

The Black Knight. *The Dial,* iii. 180 (October).

The Inward Morning. *The Dial,* iii. 198 (October). Reprinted in *A Week on the Concord and Merrimack Rivers,* p. 311.

Free Love. *The Dial,* iii. 199 (October). Reprinted in *A Week on the Concord and Merrimack Rivers,* p. 296.

The Poet's Delay. *The Dial,* iii. 200 (October). Reprinted in *A Week on the Concord and Merrimack Rivers,* p. 364.

Rumors from an Æolian Harp. *The Dial,* iii. 200 (October). Reprinted in *A Week on the Concord and Merrimack Rivers,* p. 185.

The Moon. *The Dial,* iii. 222 (October).

To the Maiden in the East. *The Dial,* iii. 222 (October). Reprinted in *A Week on the Concord and Merrimack Rivers,* p. 54.

The Summer Rain. *The Dial,* iii. 224 (October). Reprinted in *A Week on the Concord and Merrimack Rivers,* p. 320.

1843. The Laws of Menu. Selected by H. D. T. *The Dial,* iii. 331 (January).

The Prometheus Bound. Translated by H. D. T. *The Dial,* iii. 363 (January).

Anacreon. With translations. *The Dial,* iii. 484 (April). Reprinted in *A Week on the Concord and Merrimack Rivers,* p. 238.

To a Stray Fowl. *The Dial*, iii. 505 (April).

Orphics: Smoke, Haze. *The Dial*, iii. 505 (April). Reprinted in the collection of poems at the close of *Letters to Various Persons;* also, the former in *Walden*, p. 271 ; the latter in *A Week on the Concord and Merrimack Rivers*, p. 229.

Dark Ages. *The Dial*, iii. 527 (April). Reprinted in *A Week on the Concord and Merrimack Rivers*, pp. 164–168.

A Winter Walk. *The Dial*, iv. 211 (October). Reprinted in *Excursions*.

A Walk to Wachusett. *The Boston Miscellany*. Reprinted in *Excursions*.

The Landlord. *The Democratic Review*, xiii. 427 (October). Reprinted in *Excursions*.

Paradise (to be) Regained. *The Democratic Review*, xiii. 451 (November). Reprinted in *A Yankee in Canada, with Anti-Slavery and Reform Papers*.

1844. Homer, Ossian, Chaucer; extracts from a lecture on poetry, read before the Concord Lyceum, November 29, 1843. *The Dial*, iv. 290 (January).

Pindar. Translations. *The Dial*, iv. 379 (January).

Herald of Freedom. *The Dial*, iv. 507 (April). Reprinted in *A Yankee in Canada, with Anti-Slavery and Reform Papers*.

Fragments of Pindar. *The Dial*, iv. 513 (April).

1845. Wendell Phillips before the Concord Lyceum. *The Liberator*, March 28. Reprinted in *A*

Yankee in Canada, with Anti-Slavery and Reform Papers.

1847. Thomas Carlyle and his works. *Graham's Magazine,* March, April. Reprinted in *A Yankee in Canada, with Anti-Slavery and Reform Papers.*

1848. Ktaadn and the Maine Woods. *The Union Magazine.* Reprinted in *The Maine Woods.*

1849. A WEEK ON THE CONCORD AND MERRI-MACK RIVERS. Boston and Cambridge: James Munroe & Co. Reissued in 1867 by Ticknor & Fields.

Resistance to Civil Government. *Æsthetic Papers,* i. 189–211. Reprinted with the title " Civil Disobedience " in *A Yankee in Canada, with Anti-Slavery and Reform Papers.*

1853. Excursion to Canada. *Putnam's Magazine,* i. 54, 179, 321 (January, February, March). Chapters i., ii., iii., of *A Yankee in Canada.*

1854. WALDEN: OR, LIFE IN THE WOODS. Boston: Ticknor & Fields. Reissued in 1889 in two volumes, by Houghton, Mifflin & Co., in The Riverside Aldine Series.

Slavery in Massachusetts; an address delivered at the anti-slavery celebration at Framingham, Mass., July 4. *The Liberator,* July 21. Reprinted in *A Yankee in Canada, with Anti-Slavery and Reform Papers.*

1855. Cape Cod. *Putnam's Magazine,* v. 632, vi. 59, 157 (June, July, August). Chapters i.– iv. of *Cape Cod.*

1858. Chesuncook. *The Atlantic Monthly,* ii. 1,

224, 305 (June, July, August). Reprinted in
The Maine Woods.
1859. A Plea for Captain John Brown. Read to
the citizens of Concord, Mass., Sunday evening, October 30. *A Yankee in Canada, with
Anti-Slavery and Reform Papers.*
1860. Reminiscences of John Brown. Read at
North Elba, N. Y., July 4. *The Liberator*,
July 27. Reprinted with the title " The Last
Days of John Brown " in *A Yankee in Can-
ada, with Anti-Slavery and Reform Papers.*
The Succession of Forest Trees; an address
read to the Middlesex Agricultural Society
in Concord, September. *The New York
Weekly Tribune*, October 6; also in *Middle-
sex Agricultural Transactions.* Reprinted in
Excursions.
Remarks at Concord on the day of the execu-
tion of John Brown. *Echoes from Harper's
Ferry.* Boston: Thayer & Eldridge, p. 439.
1862. Walking. *The Atlantic Monthly*, ix. 657
(June). Reprinted in *Excursions.*
Autumnal Tints. *The Atlantic Monthly*, x.
385 (October). Reprinted in *Excursions.*
Wild Apples. *The Atlantic Monthly*, x. 313
(November). Reprinted in *Excursions.*
1863. Life without Principle. *The Atlantic Monthly*, xii. 484 (October). Reprinted in *A Yankee in Canada, with Anti-Slavery and Reform Papers.*
Night and Moonlight. *The Atlantic Monthly*,
xii. 579 (November). Reprinted in *Excursions.*

EXCURSIONS. (With biographical sketch by R. W. Emerson.) Boston: Ticknor & Fields.

1864. THE MAINE WOODS. (Edited by W. E. Channing.) Boston: Ticknor & Fields. N. B. — This volume contains The Allegash and East Branch, not before printed.

The Wellfleet Oysterman. *The Atlantic Monthly,* xiv. 470 (October). Reprinted in *Cape Cod.*

The Highland Light. *The Atlantic Monthly,* xiv. 649 (December). Reprinted in *Cape Cod.*

CAPE COD. (Edited by W. E. Channing.) Boston: Ticknor & Fields. [Publisher's date, 1865.]

1865. LETTERS TO VARIOUS PERSONS. (Edited by R. W. Emerson.) Boston: Ticknor & Fields.

1866. A YANKEE IN CANADA, WITH ANTI-SLAVERY AND REFORM PAPERS. (Edited by W. E. Channing.) Boston: Ticknor & Fields.

1878. April Days. *The Atlantic Monthly,* xli. 445 (April).

May Days. *The Atlantic Monthly,* xli. 567 (May).

Days in June. *The Atlantic Monthly,* xli. 711 (June). Reprinted in *Summer.*

1881. EARLY SPRING IN MASSACHUSETTS: FROM THE JOURNAL OF HENRY D. THOREAU. (Edited by H. G. O. Blake.) Boston: Houghton, Mifflin & Co.

1884. SUMMER: FROM THE JOURNAL OF HENRY

D. THOREAU. (Edited by H. G. O. Blake.) Boston: Houghton, Mifflin & Co.

1885. Winter Days. *The Atlantic Monthly*, lv. 79 (January). Reprinted in *Winter*, pp. 81-107.

1887. WINTER: FROM THE JOURNAL OF HENRY D. THOREAU. (Edited by H. G. O. Blake.) Boston: Houghton, Mifflin & Co. [Publisher's date, 1888.]

II.

BOOKS WHOLLY OR IN PART DEVOTED TO THOREAU.

1855. Duyckinck, E. A. and G. L.—*Henry D. Thoreau.* CYCLOPÆDIA OF AMERICAN LITERATURE, ii. 653–656. New York: Charles Scribner.

1857. Curtis, G. W.—*Thoreau.* HOMES OF AMERICAN AUTHORS, pp. 247–248; 250–251. New York: D. Appleton and Company.

1863. Emerson, R. W.—*Biographical Sketch.* In Thoreau's EXCURSIONS. Issued also in COMPLETE WORKS, Riverside edition, x., pp. 421–452. Boston: Houghton, Mifflin & Co.

1866. Alger, W. R.—*Thoreau.* THE SOLITUDES OF NATURE AND OF MAN. pp. 329–338. Boston: Roberts Brothers.

1868. Hawthorne, N.—PASSAGES FROM THE AMERICAN NOTE-BOOKS, ii., pp. 96–99. Boston: Ticknor & Fields.

1871. Lowell, J. R.—*Thoreau.* MY STUDY WINDOWS, pp. 193–209. Boston: James R. Osgood & Co.

1873. Channing, W. E. — THOREAU: THE POET-
NATURALIST. Boston: Roberts Brothers.

Alcott, A. B. — *Thoreau, Walden Pond.* CON-
CORD DAYS, pp. 11-20, 259-264. Boston:
Roberts Brothers.

1877. Page, H. A. (Dr. A. H. Japp). — THOREAU:
HIS LIFE AND AIMS. Boston: James R.
Osgood & Co.

1878. Sanborn, F. B. — MEMOIRS OF JOHN
BROWN, pp. 45, 49-51. Concord, Mass.

1879. Higginson, T. W. — *Thoreau.* SHORT STUD-
IES OF AMERICAN AUTHORS, pp. 23-31.
Boston: Lee & Shepard.

1880. James, Jr., H. — HAWTHORNE. *American
Men of Letters*, pp. 93-94. New York:
Harper and Brothers.

1880. Scudder, Horace E. — *Henry David Thoreau.*
AMERICAN PROSE, pp. 296-301. Boston:
Houghton. Mifflin and Co.

1881. Flagg, Wilson. — *Thoreau.* HALCYON DAYS,
pp. 164-168. Boston: Estes & Lauriat.

Cooke, G. W. — RALPH WALDO EMERSON:
HIS LIFE, WRITINGS, AND PHILOSOPHY.
(*Vide* Index.) Boston: James R. Osgood &
Co.

1882. Conway, M. D. — *Thoreau.* EMERSON AT
HOME AND ABROAD, pp. 279-289. Boston:
James R. Osgood & Co.

Alcott, A. B. — SONNETS AND CANZONETS.
Boston: Roberts Brothers.

Nichol, Prof. John. — *Thoreau.* AMERICAN
LITERATURE: AN HISTORICAL SKETCH,
pp. 313-321. Edinburgh: Adam and Charles
Black.

Welsh, A. H.— *Thoreau.* DEVELOPMENT OF
ENGLISH LITERATURE AND LANGUAGE, ii.,
pp. 409–414. Chicago: S. C. Griggs & Co.

Burroughs, John.— *Thoreau's Wildness.* ES-
SAYS FROM THE *Critic*, pp. 9–18. Boston:
James R. Osgood & Co.

Sanborn, F. B.— *Thoreau's Unpublished Poetry.* ESSAYS FROM THE *Critic*, pp. 71–78.
Boston: James R. Osgood & Co.

Sanborn, F. B.— *Reading from Thoreau's
Manuscripts.* CONCORD LECTURES ON PHI-
LOSOPHY, pp. 124–126. Cambridge: Moses
King.

1883. Sanborn, F. B.— HENRY D. THOREAU.
American Men of Letters. Boston: Houghton, Mifflin & Co.

1884. Hawthorne, Julian. — NATHANIEL HAW-
THORNE AND HIS WIFE: A BIOGRAPHY.
(*Vide* Index.) Cambridge: James R. Os-
good & Co.

1885. Sanborn, F. B.— LIFE AND LETTERS OF
JOHN BROWN. (*Vide* Index.) Boston: Roberts Brothers.

Holmes, O. W.— RALPH WALDO EMERSON.
(*Vide* Index.) *American Men of Letters.*
Boston: Houghton, Mifflin & Co.

1886. Stevenson, R. L.— *Henry David Thoreau:
His Character and Opinions.* FAMILIAR
STUDIES OF MEN AND BOOKS, pp. 129–171.
London: Chatto & Windus.

Dircks, W. H.— *Thoreau.* An Introductory
Note in WALDEN. Camelot Classics. London: Walter Scott.

Garnett, Richard. — An Introductory Note in MY STUDY WINDOWS. Camelot Classics. London: Walter Scott.

1887. Cabot, James Elliot. — A MEMOIR OF RALPH WALDO EMERSON, i., p. 282. Boston: Houghton, Mifflin & Co.

Haskins, David Green. — RALPH WALDO EMERSON: HIS MATERNAL ANCESTORS, pp. 119–122. Boston: Cupples, Upham & Co.

Whipple, E. P. — AMERICAN LITERATURE AND OTHER PAPERS, pp. 111–112. Boston: Ticknor & Co.

Beers, Prof. Henry A. — *Henry David Thoreau.* AN OUTLINE SKETCH OF AMERICAN LITERATURE, pp. 143–148. New York: Chautauqua Press.

Carpenter, Edward. — ENGLAND'S IDEAL, pp. 13–14. London: Swan, Sonnenschein, Lowrey & Co.

1888. Garnett, Richard. — LIFE OF RALPH WALDO EMERSON, pp. 157–159. Great Writers' Series. London: Walter Scott.

Besant, Walter. — THE EULOGY OF RICHARD JEFFERIES, pp. 221–225. London: Longmans, Green & Co.

Salt, H. S. — LITERARY SKETCHES. London: Swan, Sonnenschein, Lowrey & Co.

1889. Emerson, E. W. — EMERSON IN CONCORD. (*Vide* Index.) Boston: Houghton, Mifflin & Co.

Burroughs, John. — INDOOR STUDIES, pp. 1–42. Boston: Houghton, Mifflin & Co.

Dircks, W. H.—*Thoreau.* A Preparatory Note in A WEEK ON THE CONCORD AND MERRIMAC [*sic*] RIVERS, pp. v–xviii. Camelot Classics. London: Walter Scott.

Frothingham, O. B.—*Thoreau, Henry David.* CYCLOPÆDIA OF AMERICAN BIOGRAPHY, vi., pp. 100–101. New York: D. Appleton and Company.

Hubert, Jr., Philip G.—*Henry David Thoreau.* LIBERTY AND A LIVING, pp. 171–190. New York and London: G. P. Putnam's Sons.

1890. Jones, Dr. S. A.—THOREAU: A GLIMPSE. WITH A BIBLIOGRAPHY. Ann Arbor: No publisher.

Ellis, Havelock.—THE NEW SPIRIT, pp. 90–99. London: George Bell & Sons.

Charles J. Woodbury.—*Thoreau.* TALKS WITH RALPH WALDO EMERSON, pp. 69–94. London: Kegan Paul, Trench, Trübner & Co., Ltd.

The same. New York: Baker & Taylor Co.

Salt, H. S.—THE LIFE OF HENRY DAVID THOREAU. London: Richard Bentley & Son.

III.

MAGAZINE ARTICLES.

1849. George Ripley.—A Week on the Concord and Merrimack Rivers. *The New York Tribune.*

J. R. Lowell.—A Week on the Concord and Merrimack Rivers. *Massachusetts Quarterly Review,* iii., ix. (December), 40–51.

A Week on the Concord and Merrimack Rivers. *Athenæum* (October 27).

1854. A. P. Peabody. — Walden : or Life in the Woods. *North American Review*, lxxix. 536.

C. F. Briggs. — A Yankee Diogenes. *Putnam's Magazine*, iv. 443.

1855. Edwin Morton. — Thoreau and his Books. *The Harvard Magazine*, i. No. ii. (January), 87–99. [*Vide* Sanborn's *Thoreau*. "American Men of Letters," pp. 195–199.]

A Rural Humbug. *Knickerbocker Magazine*, xlv. 235.

1857. An American Diogenes. *Chambers' Edinburgh Journal*, xxviii. 330.

1862. G. W. Curtis. — Reminiscences of Thoreau. *Harper's Magazine*, xxv. 270.

R. W. Emerson. — Thoreau. *Atlantic Monthly*, x. 239.

1864. T. W. Higginson. — The Maine Woods. *Atlantic Monthly*, xiv. 386.

The Transcendentalists of Concord. *Fraser's Magazine*, lxx. 245. [Same article in *Eclectic Magazine*, lxiii. 231 ; *Littell's Living Age*, lxxxiii. 99, 178.]

An American Rousseau. *Saturday Review* (December 3).

1865. T. W. Higginson. — Cape Cod. *Atlantic Monthly*, xv. 381.

T. W. Higginson. — Letters to Various Persons. *Atlantic Monthly*, xvi. 504.

J. A. Weiss. — Thoreau. *Christian Examiner*, lxxix. 96.

W. R. Alger. — Thoreau. *Monthly Religious Magazine*, xxxv. 382.

M. D. Conway. — Thoreau. *Fraser's Magazine*, lxxiii. 447. [Same article in *Eclectic Magazine*, lxvii. 180 (1886); *Every Saturday*, i. 622 (1886).]

J. R. Lowell. — "Letters to Various Persons." By Henry D. Thoreau. *North American Review*, ci. 597.

1869. G. W. Curtis. — Further Reminiscences of Thoreau. *Harper's Magazine*, xxxviii. 415.

1870. J. R. Lowell. — Thoreau. *Every Saturday*, x. 166.

1873. Thoreau. *British Quarterly*, lix. 181. [Same article in *Littell's Living Age*, cxx. 643: *Eclectic Magazine*, lxxxii. 305.]

1874. Henry Thoreau, the Poet-Naturalist. *British Quarterly* (January).

Ellery Channing's Thoreau. *The Nation* (January 8).

1875. Miss H. R. Hudson. — Concord Books. *Harper's Magazine*, li. 18.

1877. M. Collins. — Thoreau. *Dublin University Magazine*, xc. 610.

T. Hughes. — Study of Thoreau. *Eclectic Magazine*, xc. 114.

Theodore Watts. — Article in *Athenæum* (November 17).

1878. J. V. O'Connor. — Henry D. Thoreau and New England Transcendentalism. *Catholic World*, xxvii. 289.

1879. The Pity and Humor of Thoreau. *Littell's Living Age*, cxlvi. 190.

R. L. Stevenson. — Henry David Thoreau : His Character and Opinions. *Cornhill Magazine*, xli. 665. [Same article in *Littell's Living Age*, cxlvi. 179; *Eclectic Magazine*, xcv. 257 (1880).]

1880. W. S. Kennedy. — A New Estimate of Henry D. Thoreau. *Penn Monthly*, xi. 794.

Philosophy at Concord. *The Nation* (September 2).

W. S. Kennedy. — A New Estimate of Thoreau. *Penn Monthly*, ii. 794.

1881. Thoreau's Portrait. By himself. *The Literary World* (Boston), xii. 116–117 (March 26).

F. B. Sanborn. — Henry David Thoreau. *The Harvard Register*, iii. 214–217 (April). *Portrait.*

1882. John Burroughs. — Henry D. Thoreau. *The Century*, ii. (New Series). 368.

John Burroughs. — Thoreau's Wildness. *Critic*, i. 74.

F. B. Sanborn. — Thoreau's Unpublished Poetry. *Critic*, i. 75.

Portraits of Thoreau with a Beard. *Critic*, i. 95.

Henry D. Thoreau : Sanborn's Life of. *The Nation*, xxxv. 34.

Henry D. Thoreau : Sanborn's Life of. *Literary World* (Boston), xiii. 227.

Henry D. Thoreau : Sanborn's Life of. *Athenæum*, ii. (of the year), 558.

J. A. Janvier. — Henry D. Thoreau : Sanborn's Life of. *American*, iv. 218.

Henry D. Thoreau : Sanborn's Life of. *Academy*, ii. 271.

Theodore Watts. — Article in *Athenæum* (October 28).

1883. H. N. Powers. — H. D. Thoreau. *Dial* (Chicago), iii. 70.

Henry D. Thoreau. *Spectator*, lvi. 239.

1884. Walter Lewin. — "Summer: From the Journal of Henry D. Thoreau." *The Nation*, xxvi. 193.

"Summer: From the Journal of Henry D. Thoreau." *Literary World* (Boston), xv. 223.

1885. Henry D. Thoreau. *Spectator*, lviii. 122.

J. Benton. — Thoreau's Poetry. *Lippincott's Magazine*, xxxvii. 491.

G. Willis Cooke. — The Dial. *Journal of Speculative Philosophy* (July).

1886. H. S. Salt. — Henry D. Thoreau. *Temple Bar*, lxxviii. 369. Reprinted, 1888, in *Literary Sketches*, by H. S. Salt. London: Swan, Sonnenschein, Lowrey & Co.

1887. H. S. Salt. — Henry D. Thoreau. *Eclectic Magazine*, cviii. 89.

H. S. Salt. — Henry D. Thoreau. *The Critic*, ii. 276, 289. From *Temple Bar*.

A. H. Japp. — Henry David Thoreau. *The Welcome* (November).

1888. Henry D. Thoreau. *Good Words*, xxix. 445.

Grant Allen. — A Sunday at Concord. *Fortnightly Review* (May).

1889. John Burroughs. — Henry D. Thoreau. *Chautauquan*, ix. 530.

"Week on the Concord and Merrimack Rivers." *Saturday Review*, lxviii. 195.

1890. S. A. Jones. — Thoreau: A Glimpse. *The Unitarian*, v. 2, 3, 4 (February, March, April).

H. S. Salt. — Thoreau's Poetry. *The Art Review* (London), i. 5 (May).

C. J. Woodbury. — Emerson's Talks with a College Boy. *The Century* (February).

INDEX.

———◆———

INDEX.

Marriage, both common and divine sense should be consulted in, 57.

Marriages, the rarity of real, 56.

Melancholy, yield not to, in the upward path, 51.

Men, and beasts, delicacy of the distinction between, 9; ask too seldom to be nobly dealt with, 31; may punish us for satisfying God, 64; the limited views of, 98.

Mind, an adventure in the, rather than in the thing done, 80; not to be desecrated by gossip and affairs, 101; let your, be open to the best, 102.

Money, not necessary for the soul, 27; the evil of earning, *merely*, 95.

Moods, work in spite of, 72.

Moral quality of nature and life, the, 8.

Morning, the invitation of, 14; is whenever we are truly awake, 15.

Mortality and immortality, 20.

Mountains, the, within us, 77.

Muse, the, should lead, the understanding follow, 49; too plaintive, 110.

Music, you hear, step to the, 24; exalting effect of, 41; the significance of, 108; the sound of the universal laws promulgated, 108; has no history, 115.

Nature, our double, 3; sympathy of, with the human race, 5; the moral quality of, and life, 8; friendship and the love of, harmonize, 40; friendship in, 53; humanity before, 74; poverty of outward, 77; prevails over man in a large landscape, 89; no poetry so wild as, 91; a border life between society and, 92; vision through the works of man to the wildness of, 93; few speak simply enough of, 106; the promise in the face of, 119; no book can match, 120; on the side of what is best in us, 123.

Necessaries, providing, a pleasure, 69.

Neighbor, our nearest, 3.

Neighborhood, the best, 2.

News, as compared with eternal truth, the, 17; the kind of, we really want, 50.

Newspaper, life sacrificed to the, 100; a world outside of the, 100.

Newspapers, 48.

Noble, the offspring of the, tend to a higher nobility, 63.

Obscurity above better than false clearness below, 68.

Offspring of the noble tend to a higher nobility, 63.

Out-door life, 94.

Palate, inspiration through the, 8.

Path, a person irresistible on his own, 28.

Perception, the joy of love and of intellectual, 62.

"Plain living and high thinking," 17.

Poet, the hibernation of the, 105.

Poetry, no, so wild as nature, 91; the authorship of, 104.

Polishing the world, 71.

Postponement, fatal, 75.

Poverty, need not take from us the purest enjoyments, 26; advantage of, 27; inward, 52; of nature and internal wealth, 77.

Present, living in the, 22.

Problem of life, simplify the, 42; wealth complicates the, 63.

Prospect, the interest of a new, 89.

Purification of a soul gives it a new life, the, 11.

Purity, inspires the soul, 9; and sensuality each a single thing, 10.

Purpose, singleness of, 119.

Reader, there must be good hearing to make a good, 112.

Reading, the best kind of, 1.

Reality, what alone has, 18; the great, is ever here and now, 18; seek to penetrate through surfaces to, 19; our faintest dream points to the solidest, 43.

Realm within, the glory of the, 23.

Reform, individual life the true source of, 44; is better than its modes, 44.